STORIES I TELL MYSELF

Hunter pointing out to me the skill of his shooting, somewhere in a California forest, 1964. He is holding his .44 Magnum, probably his favorite gun.

STORIES I TELL MYSELF

Growing Up with Hunter S. Thompson

JUAN F. THOMPSON

Alfred A. Knopf New York 2016

Library of Congress Cataloging-in-Publication Data
Thompson, Juan F.
Stories I tell myself : growing up with Hunter S. Thompson /
Juan F. Thompson. — First United States edition.
pages cm
ISBN 978-0-307-26535-7 (hardcover) — ISBN 978-1-101-87586-5 (eBook)
1. Thompson, Hunter S. 2. Thompson, Hunter S.—Family. 3. Authors,
American—20th century—Biography. 4. Thompson, Juan F. I. Title.
PS3570.H62Z89 2015
813'.54—dc23
[B]
2015006934

With deepest gratitude to my wife, Jennifer Winkel Thompson, and to Deb Fuller, who together showed me my father's hidden language of love. It has made all the difference.

To my son, Will, whom I have loved with all my heart from the moment he was born, and will always love without condition or limit.

FORGIVING OUR FATHERS

Dick Lourie

for M.K.

maybe in a dream: he's in your power
you twist his arm but you're not sure it was
he that stole your money   you feel calmer
and you decide to let him go free

or he's the one (as in a dream of mine)
I must pull from the water but I never
knew it or wouldn't have done it until
I saw the street-theater play so close up
I was moved to actions I'd never before taken

maybe for leaving us too often or
forever when we were little   maybe
for scaring us with unexpected rage
or making us nervous because there seemed
never to be any rage there at all

for marrying or not marrying our mothers
for divorcing or not divorcing our mothers
and shall we forgive them for their excesses
of warmth or coldness   shall we forgive them

for pushing or leaning for shutting doors
for speaking only through layers of cloth
or never speaking or never being silent

in our age or in theirs or in their deaths
saying it to them or not saying it—
if we forgive our fathers what is left

CONTENTS

Preface

THIS IS A MEMOIR, not a biography, a highly subjective and unreliable memoir of how my father and I got to know each other over forty-one years until his suicide in 2005. It is filled with exaggerations, misstatements, faulty recollections, obfuscations, omissions, and elisions. It also contains a lot of truth about my father and me, more truth than falsehoods, I think.

If I am deceiving you, though, I am deceiving myself first of all. It's just that all I have is memory, and memory is a treacherous thing, treacherous, as in unfaithful and perfidious. Double-crossing and underhanded. Memory is not objective. It is not an impartial recorder, but instead a selective, changeable, and unreliable record being constantly revised and edited to suit our needs and desires. Yet our lives and our identities are largely built upon our memories, and we trust them implicitly so we can draw our conclusions about our lives and the people in them. So we do the best we can, knowing we are fooling ourselves a good part of our lives. We go forward in spite of it. I go forward in spite of it. These are the stories I tell myself.

Hunter S. Thompson was a complex man, far too complex for

me to completely know or understand. He was famous, almost worshipped in some circles, unknown in others, brilliant, a grand master of the written word and one of the great writers of the twentieth century. He was an alcoholic and drug fiend, a wild, angry, passionate, sometimes dangerous, charismatic, unpredictable, irresponsible, idealistic, sensitive man with a powerful and deeply rooted sense of justice. Most important to me, though, he was my father and I was his son. And no son can escape the claim of that relationship. Good or bad, weak or strong, alive or dead, close or distant, our fathers are with us. This is the story of how my father and I went very far away from each other, and over twenty-five years managed to find our way back before it was too late.

Stories I Tell Myself

ONE

My Father as a Young Man

"Nothing but a smart hillbilly"—The Air Force or jail—
The writing life: New York, San Francisco, Big Sur,
Aspen—Partying with Ken Kesey and the Hells Angels
motorcycle gang—Elk liver in an unheated shack

A STORY NEEDS a starting place. In this story, the starting place is my father's early life, because he, like everyone,
was to some degree a product of his upbringing. The very brief
biographical sketch that follows is intended to familiarize those
readers who haven't heard of him before and to lay out some
essentials of his early life before and following my birth in 1964.

Hunter was born and raised in Louisville, Kentucky. His family had been in Kentucky for generations, and there are names
like Semeranis Lawless and America Hook in our Thompson
family tree. He sometimes called himself "nothing but a smart
hillbilly." He was born in 1937 and had two brothers, Davison
and Jim, both younger. His father was an insurance salesman,
and his mother was a stay-at-home mom until his father died

suddenly when he was a teenager and she had to go to work. He attended public school, read constantly, spent time with the children of Louisville's Old Money families, and scraped through high school not due to lack of intelligence but because of boredom and hostility to authority. He also got into a fair amount of trouble, so that at age seventeen he spent thirty days in the county jail for a bogus petty robbery charge. It would have been sixty days except the judge gave him the option of joining the Air Force in return for the reduced sentence.

He enlisted and was initially trained to be a radio technician. He despised everything about the military and probably would have spent four years in solitary confinement for chronic and unrepentant insubordination if he hadn't managed to lie his way into a job as the sports editor for the base newspaper, *The Command Courier.* This made all the difference. He worked his own hours (slept late, worked late), came and went as he pleased, did unauthorized freelance writing for a local civilian paper, and wrote entertaining, flattering, and wildly exaggerated articles about the base sports teams. This curried favor with the base commander, who in turn excused Hunter from the customary airman duties and shielded him from the constant complaints of other officers. In this way he survived three years of the Air Force, got an early honorable discharge, and gained some solid experience as a journalist. He also understood that he wanted to be a writer, and a damn good one. Not a journalist, but a novelist, like Hemingway or Fitzgerald.

Hunter fully intended to go to college as soon as he was out of the Air Force on a journalism scholarship. Somewhere along the line, though, that became less important, and he never did attend college, with the exception of a couple of night classes at Columbia University in New York in 1959. He told me much later that he realized that in order to be a great writer he needed to write, not go to school. After I had graduated from college, he said the only reason to attend college was to have four years to read.

After his discharge, he held a couple of brief jobs on newspapers on the East Coast, including a stint as a copy boy at *Time* magazine. He was either fired from or quit each of these jobs, and soon realized he would never be able to work in an office for a boss, that he wasn't wired for it. It became clear to him that working as a salaried journalist was not going to allow him to be the kind of writer that he wanted to be. So, he became a freelance journalist, at starvation wages, but with the freedom to work on his own terms.

Not that he was lazy. He worked hard on his first novel, *Prince Jellyfish* (never published), cranked out freelance articles, and wrote a vast number of letters to friends around the country. He looked at letter writing as not only a way to keep in touch and debate ideas, but as a writing exercise, so that when he wasn't sleeping or in the bar with friends, he was writing. He moved constantly, went through a long string of old and worn-out cars, slept during the day and worked at night, borrowed money (and lent it when he had it), stayed one step ahead of the bill collectors, and left a trail of small-time debt across the country. He also kept carbon copies of everything he wrote in neatly organized and carefully labeled folders.

In New York City he met my mother, and then spent several months traveling around South America as a freelancer for *The Nation* and *The National Observer,* a weekly paper published by Dow Jones. He and my mother lived in Puerto Rico for a while (which provided the raw material for his first and only published novel, *The Rum Diary*), got married and headed west to California, lived in Big Sur for a bit, headed to a happening place in the

Colorado Rockies called Aspen that some friends had just discovered, spent a year or so there, then returned to the San Francisco Bay Area in 1963.

I was born in March of 1964. At that time Hunter and Sandy were living in an unheated shack in Glen Ellen, California, about sixty miles north of San Francisco. He was traveling quite a bit, freelancing for several newspapers and magazines and making hardly any money. My mother did secretarial work, providing a minimal steady paycheck to compensate for Hunter's irregular freelance income. For food, he would occasionally shoot a deer or an elk. My mother told me that for the duration of her pregnancy she lived on elk meat (especially elk liver), salad, and milk.

Hunter and Sandy on the tarmac in Bermuda in
1960 with his typewriter, pipe, and horsewhip

*Hunter, Sandy, and me in the front yard of
the shack in Glen Ellen, California, 1964*

Six months after my birth, we moved from Glen Ellen to
318 Parnassus Avenue in San Francisco near Golden Gate Park,
where Hunter wrote a big chunk of *Hell's Angels,* a book-length
nonfiction account of the several months he spent with the infamous motorcycle gang in 1965. The Angels had been getting a
lot of sensational press in the mid-1960s in which they were represented as evil, crazy thugs determined to destroy everything
good and right in America. Hunter was curious to know the real
story, and proposed that he write a magazine article on the Hells
Angels. He ended up spending around six months with the Oak-
land chapter, not as a member but as a journalist who wanted
to know their story. Though he ended up getting stomped by
the gang for allegedly betraying the terms of the financial deal
he had with them, he had gotten the material he needed. In his
book he portrays them as neither devils nor revolutionaries but
as mostly small-time hoodlums and drifters with very limited

Hunter teaching me to swim, 1964

options, unallied to any ideology or greater movement. Though the book was nonfiction, it wasn't purely objective. It was a story about Hunter and the Hells Angels and how he met them, dealt with them, rode with them, and learned about them, from his point of view.

Hell's Angels was published in 1966. It got good reviews and sold well. Hunter would remain a freelance journalist and author his whole life, and in the eight years from 1966 to 1974, he wrote the three books that cemented his reputation as one of the great American writers: *Hell's Angels, Fear and Loathing in Las Vegas,* and *Fear and Loathing on the Campaign Trail '72.*

While Hunter was traveling and working, my mother kept the family ship steady with her conventional day job that paid the rent and bought the food. However, now and then Hunter would bring my mother and me into his world. He had crossed paths with Ken Kesey, a noted writer and drug enthusiast who was known for throwing wild parties at his place in the woods south of San Francisco. The two of them thought it would be a good idea to invite the Hells Angels to one of Kesey's parties, and naturally my mother went along and brought me. I can only imagine the scene: dozens, maybe hundreds of people in various stages of undress, stoned on pot, tripping on LSD, drunk on beer—maybe all three at once—wandering around in the forest while music blared from the house and the colored lights strung among the trees flashed. At one point during the party the Hells Angels gang-raped a woman in a small cabin, an event that haunted Hunter for a long time afterward. In the midst of the madness, there I was, maybe a year old, maybe younger, asleep in a corner

*In the family lederhosen running through the
San Francisco Zoo, circa 1967*

With Sandy in California, 1964

of one of the cabins, absorbing wild sense-impressions, probably safe enough but in a situation that violates all my notions of safe and responsible parenting.

In 1970, Hunter covered the Kentucky Derby for a short-lived magazine called *Scanlan's* and wrote what turned out to be his first piece of Gonzo journalism, a word coined by a fellow writer to describe Hunter's unique combination of first-person subjectivity, factual reporting, and hyperbole written in raw, powerful prose. The word "Gonzo" eventually became synonymous with both Hunter's writing and his lifestyle.

His next book, *Fear and Loathing in Las Vegas,* stemming from an assignment for *Rolling Stone,* was Gonzo taken to new heights. Not quite fiction, not quite nonfiction, very funny, but with serious themes, it is ostensibly the story of my father's and his attorney's adventures while under the influence of many different drugs, all told from Hunter's very subjective point of view. This book established his reputation as a master of satire as well as an unapologetic consumer of an impossible quantity and variety of drugs.

Two years later, he wrote *Fear and Loathing on the Campaign Trail '72,* also a subjective story of his experiences covering the 1972 presidential campaign. As he wrote in the preface, he didn't intend to write a factual account of the campaign. Instead, he wanted to capture what it was like to be in the campaign, capture essential truths that so-called objective journalism cannot grasp, and then write about it without concern for alienating sources or contacts, since he had no intention of becoming a Washington political correspondent. This book showed Hunter to be an extremely perceptive observer of American politics and a deeply idealistic man who wrote passionately and fearlessly about the real and foul nature of politics and politicians.

However, the persona that took root and flourished over the next forty years was that of the drug-crazed Wild Man of journalism, more rebel hoodlum than iconoclast, more buffoon than satirist. He was portrayed as such by Bill Murray in the 1980 movie *Where the Buffalo Roam.* In 1998 Terry Gilliam directed Johnny Depp in a film adaptation of *Fear and Loathing in Las Vegas,* which, though it did capture more of the complexities of the book, still presented Hunter primarily as a drug fiend and mischief-maker.

Which he was. He was an alcoholic, drug addict, and a hell-raiser, but he was also a brilliant writer and craftsman of the language, facts that are still overshadowed by his Wild Man persona. This is the persona most people think of when they hear the name Hunter S. Thompson, if they know the name at all. And that is a shame. He was first and always a writer in the best and highest sense of the word, in which writing is a vocation, not an occupation. Everything else was secondary. Drugs, family, lovers, friends, sex, adventure, they all came after writing. And into his world I came in 1964, when he was twenty-seven, poor, and living in an unheated shack with his new bride.

TWO

Memories Begin: ages 2 to 10

Owl Farm—The Success of Hell's Angels*—Early working
habits—Guns, motorcycles, friends in the kitchen—The
Jerome Bar—Washington, D.C., the Free School*

HST TIMELINE

1966   *Hell's Angels* published. Hunter, Sandy, and Juan move back to
Aspen.

1968   HST on Nixon press bus during 1968 presidential campaign.
Hunter buys house and 140 acres of land in Woody Creek from
George Stranahan.
HST at Democratic National Convention in Chicago during
the riots.

1969   Involved in Joe Edwards's run for mayor of Aspen, fall
1969—Hunter becomes interested in the potential of the
disaffected Youth Vote (Freak Power) to change local and
national politics.
Hunter meets Jann Wenner, publisher of *Rolling Stone* magazine,
in San Francisco.

1970   Writes "The Kentucky Derby Is Decadent and Depraved"
for *Scanlan's* magazine, which was the first example of Gonzo
journalism. Hunter and Ralph Steadman work together for the
first time.
Writes "Freak Power in the Rockies" for *Rolling Stone.*
Hunter runs for sheriff in Aspen and loses by a very slim
margin. End of Freak Power.

MY EARLY MEMORIES are like photographs, freeze-frame images disconnected from any sense of time or continuity, as if the photos in an album were thrown up in the air and fell randomly, some facedown, invisible, some faceup, and all of them completely out of sequence and context. There are also those memories that are based on stories I've been told. I wasn't there, I just imagined the scene, and it became a memory, another snapshot in the pile, indistinguishable from a real memory. For instance, I remember my mother in a long sheepskin coat embroidered with multicolored thread standing outside a cabin in Woody Creek in the winter, surrounded by a couple of feet of snow. Is this a real memory? Or one of many snapshots in one of the many family photo albums? I don't know. Whatever their source, however, my early memories, scattered and unreliable as they are, are tinged with a warm hazy glow, and I treasure them.

When we first came to Colorado as a family in 1966, before Hunter bought Owl Farm, we lived in a rented old farmhouse in Woody Creek, a narrow mountain valley about ten miles outside of Aspen. It was then primarily a ranching community with lots of Hereford cattle, hay and clover fields, and a house every half mile or so. Though Aspen was beginning to transform into a cosmopolitan ski resort, Woody Creek stayed far behind, still maintaining the rural ranching lifestyle that had taken root in the late 1800s when Aspen was a mining boomtown.

Not everyone in Woody Creek was a rancher, however. George

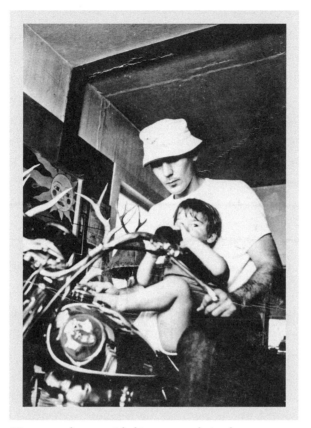

*Hunter and me astride his motorcycle in the apartment
on Parnassus Avenue in San Francisco, 1965*

Stranahan, scion of a wealthy family and a physics professor at
Carnegie Mellon University, bought up a good chunk of the middle Woody Creek Valley in the 1950s. He and his family would
live there for the next fifty years. He was Hunter's first landlord
in Woody Creek, eventually sold him Owl Farm, and was one of
his political allies for decades to come.

Our farmhouse was right off the Lenado Road on Stranahan's

ranch. The three of us lived there for a year or so. There was an old barn and a horse pen right across the driveway, and a shack next to the house that may have been a bunkhouse at one time, and which Hunter used as his writing office. I remember my room was upstairs, up a short staircase from Hunter and Sandy's bedroom to what had once been an attic. It was cozy and bright. I remember our red-and-white '57 Chevy with the big bench seat out in the driveway, and the deep snow everywhere, especially deep to a two-year-old. If the number of photos from that time is any indication, Hunter was very pleased to be a father. I have several photos of Hunter holding my infant self, balancing me on his knee, Hunter and Sandy sitting over me as I baked in the spring sunshine, and Hunter holding me in a swimming pool. My favorite is a photo of Hunter standing beside a large tree with a target nailed to it, a .44 Magnum pistol in one hand and a tiny me in his other arm, pointing with the barrel of the gun at the tight grouping of shots in the center of the target.

He was often on the other side of the camera. When he was a young freelance writer, he was by necessity a photographer as well as a writer, and apparently he frequently turned his camera on me. There are pictures of me as a baby in Glen Ellen, and then in San Francisco—in a playground, at a party, on the sidewalk, in a streetcar. There is a self-portrait of Hunter holding me while sitting on his Norton motorcycle in our apartment on Parnassus Avenue. In Colorado, there are pictures of me playing in the snow at our first house, me with our Dobermans, Darwin and Benjy. There are photos of me on a tractor, swinging on a tire swing, and a bit later, me posing with Hunter in a Groucho Marx mask.

• • •

THERE ARE MANY PHOTOS from over the years that I discovered while going through the hundreds of boxes that make up my father's archive, which contains everything from manuscripts and reporter's notebooks to junk mail, to-do lists from twenty-five years ago, and canceled checks from 1964.

I don't remember him taking these photographs. I don't remember these events. By the time my memories really kick in around six or seven, Hunter was a background presence, but not a part of my daily life. He seemed to live roughly in parallel with my mother and me without being a part of the family. He slept, he wrote, he traveled frequently, he spent a lot of time with friends in Aspen, and he ran for sheriff, among many other things. I don't remember him spending time with me, between his vampire schedule, his friends, and his ambition as a writer.

My consistent memories begin at Owl Farm, a split-log ranch-style house that he bought from Stranahan in 1968, and where he lived continuously until his death. During the school year I remember Sandy waking me up in the dark, and me stumbling to the bathroom where I would curl up on the red shag carpet in front of the heater vent and go into a half sleep until Sandy came to tell me to get dressed and to come eat breakfast. I always ate at the kitchen counter—Hunter had not yet established that spot as his writing place. Then I would go into the living room and watch through the huge picture windows that overlooked the upper Woody Creek Valley and the Lenado Road that ran in front of our house. I was watching for the school bus to come around the corner by the Craig ranch about a mile up the road. As soon as it appeared I would hurry into my coat and boots and run down the driveway to the road and get on the short yellow bus. Hunter would be sound asleep most of the day. By the time I returned at around three p.m. he would usually still be sleeping. While Hunter was sleeping there was to be quiet. Around four or four-thirty in the afternoon Sandy would wake him, and he would shamble into the kitchen in his bathrobe and take his place at the kitchen counter in time for the *CBS Evening News* with Walter Cronkite on our black-and-white television, which received only one channel. I remember every night there were solemn reports from the Vietnam War. Sandy would make breakfast for him, always bacon and eggs, often with corned beef hash, and some toast with orange marmalade. Hunter would read the newspaper and watch the news while he ate. Sometimes this was dinner for me also, or sometimes my dinner would come later. We never ate as a family. After breakfast, Hunter would take a shower, get dressed, and begin his day. This usually meant head-

Hunter's photo of Agar, his Doberman at the time, facing off against the head of a deer Hunter had shot. Sandy is in the background, pregnant with me, circa 1963.

*Hunter took this photo of me
playing with Tinkertoys on the floor
in 1966 in the Stranahans' cabin,
before we moved to Owl Farm.*

ing out to see a friend or driving into Aspen. I would not see him until the next afternoon, for he would make the rounds of his friends at night, and then if he was going to write, he would start long after I was in bed and asleep. Weekends were tricky because of the prime directive to stay quiet and not wake up Hunter. I would get up for Saturday cartoons nice and early, curl up in a blanket on the couch in the kitchen, eat a box of chocolate or peanut butter Space Food Sticks, and watch TV until about nine or ten, when the boring big-kid shows came on, then find something to do, either read or play by myself. Sandy would rise usu-

With Hunter on the front porch at Owl Farm in 1969.
He was using the TarGard for his cigarettes even then.

ally late morning, and Hunter would be on his usual schedule, waking up in the late afternoon.

The summers in the early '70s, before my parents' marriage began to visibly crumble, were long and sweet. I especially remember summer picnics up in Little Woody Creek, a small valley that shoots off the main Woody Creek Valley, where some good friends of my parents' lived, and who had children about my age. Nobody seemed to have traditional nine-to-five jobs. Sometimes Hunter would crank up his Bultaco Matador trail motorcycle, I would climb on the back and hang on to him as tightly as I could, and we would race down the street, turn onto the dirt Little Woody Creek Road, and roar up the little valley trailing a big cloud of dust. I remember Hunter's broad back, my little hands clutching his coat because I couldn't reach all the way around his body, and how even though it seemed like we were on the verge of a horrible accident, I trusted him. When we arrived at our destination I was buzzing from both the adrenaline and the vibration of the motorcycle. We never talked about it, it was just a quick motorcycle ride, but it was also a private adventure just between us. We didn't have that many of them, so those memories are precious.

The summer before Hunter died, I took my son, Will, who was six, for a ride on Hunter's BMW R75/5 motorcycle. I started out slowly, concerned that he would react as I had done, that he would be afraid of speed. As we idled down the road at fifteen miles per hour, I asked him how he was doing. He said, "Good!"

Hunter and the posse in the Jerome Bar in 1970

I went a bit faster, and checked again. "Good!" he said. I had planned on just going a couple of hundred feet up the road and then coming back, but his evident enthusiasm led me to keep going up the road, all the way to where the pavement ends. On the way back to Owl Farm, he leaned forward and said, "Faster, Daddy!" I think we hit sixty before I had to slow down to make the turn into the driveway.

There were two families up in Little Woody that we were especially close with, the LeFavours and the Smiths. John Smith was the head of the tiny local community television station called Grassroots. He had a wife, Katy, and two children, Nicholas and Emily, who were around my age. They had come from out west, where John had been a professor of journalism at UCLA. He had opted out of academia to start and run Grassroots based on the idea that television should not be controlled solely by corporations. The Smiths' house was down by the Little Woody Creek, and the banks were thick with willows and grass. Hunter and I would arrive on the motorcycle on a hot day in the summer. There were already a few other families there; Hunter was never the first to arrive. I would find the other kids, and Hunter would join the adults, who would re-form around him. When Hunter arrived at a gathering, he never joined a group, he became the focus of the group. Without effort, he simply commanded everyone's attention. His mother, Virginia, once told me that even when he was a little boy, eating breakfast before school, there were other little boys waiting outside on the sidewalk, waiting to walk with him to school, not because he bribed them, or flattered them, or threatened them, only because they wanted to be near him.

I remember watermelon, hot dogs, soda pop, and a little

bridge across the creek. There was an open outhouse hidden by the bushes, which consisted of a wide board with a hole cut in it over a hole in the ground. I don't know if the adults used it, but that's what the kids used. The hot sunny days eased into warm summer evenings, the adults talking and laughing in groups as the sun went down over the mesa, the children playing in the creek or in the little aspen grove that grew alongside it. I think we all were happy then, so that we didn't even think about being happy. It was all right, the children, the twilight, the friends, the blue sky darkening to indigo, the laughter—it was all right in that way you don't notice until you look back much later and realize you were happy then.

The LeFavours, Bruce and Pat and their two daughters, Nicole and Cree, lived at the very end of Little Woody Road, past the Smiths. Bruce and Pat were both gourmet chefs who owned a fine French restaurant in Aspen, the Paragon. Their house and

Me on the front porch of Owl Farm around 1970

land were a little Garden of Eden. Bruce had designed and built the house. They owned dozens of acres at the end of the valley, at the end of a narrow dirt road. There was a little pond on one side of the road and a small tack shed for the two Shetland ponies. On the left was what may have been a scraggly and neglected orchard, or perhaps just a grove of scrub oak from which the underbrush had been cleared so that long grass grew in the shade beneath. The road wound along the side of the hill for a bit, then crossed over the creek and up to the house. A forest of aspen trees filled the space to the top of the valley, and steeply up each side rose the red walls of the mountains, looming, blocking the sun for all but the middle of the day, but also allowing plants and trees to grow that could not thrive in the sharp bright heat of the high-altitude sun.

The house itself was two stories and covered with white stucco, with thick brown timbers. In my memory it had a turret on one side, a huge dark wooden front door, and smallish windows set deep into the walls, something like a very small castle for a minor lord. A castle nonetheless, because it was lovely in its solitude among the aspen trees, at the very end of the valley, the nearest house a good mile or two away. The space surrounding it and the lush growth along the creek were extravagant in an unconscious, unplanned way that I just took for granted, and I imagine all of us who grew up in Woody Creek did. The space, the deep blue mountain skies, the contrasts of the snow on the fourteen-thousand-foot peaks with the bright reddish orange of the iron oxide bluffs in Woody Creek, the tall grass by the streams, it was just the place where we grew up.

I think it was a good time for Hunter as well. His years of hard work as a freelance writer had paid off, he had written two excellent books, *Hell's Angels* and *Fear and Loathing in Las Vegas,* and was working on his third, *Fear and Loathing on the Campaign Trail '72.* He had a growing fame as both a writer and an "outlaw journalist." He had his home, Owl Farm, he had a devoted wife and a healthy young son, and he had friends—lots of friends, good friends, smart friends. I think he had friends for every kind of adventure or conversation, a skill or habit that is evident from his earliest letters up to his last days. National politics, local politics, literature, sex, art, the media, journalism, football, gambling, driving, motorcycles, drugs, photography, these were all topics that he loved, and he had friends for each. He roamed around Aspen and Woody Creek like it was his private club, and in those days his headquarters was without question the Hotel Jerome Bar.

*Hunter and Oscar Zeta Acosta during
Hunter's run for sheriff of Aspen in 1970*

Center of the Eye Photography Studio, Aspen, 1970

I can't tell you what it was like to be an adult at the Jerome, what it was like when Hunter held court from the end of the bar, but I can tell you how the bar appeared to a child. It was loud with music and laughing, hooting, yelling, a cacophony of conversations, and it smelled like beer, the distinctive smell of an old bar, the sharp, slightly sweet, slightly acrid smell of cigarettes and beer. It was crowded with people on the bar stools, between the stools, at the tables, and everywhere in between, though as a child I learned to snake through the narrow spaces between the adults so that they hardly noticed me.

ONE NIGHT I discovered that drunk people drop money on the floor. I began crawling under the bar stools, picking up dimes, nickels, and quarters. I couldn't believe I hadn't noticed this simple source of income earlier. I realized that at one stool there were more coins each time I passed. I looked up and saw a man looking down at me, laughing and dropping them. I gathered up the money and took my booty down to Carl's Pharmacy at the end of the block to buy Archie comic books.

I remember Hunter at the end of the bar facing the door, standing, never sitting, always smoking a cigarette, listening with his head bent down, brow furrowed, or speaking, his eyes, his whole body commanding attention, and his smile. He was holding court. When Hunter took up his position at the bar, he got the day's news, delivered his opinions, praised this per-

*In our front yard at Owl Farm in 1971 or so, with our
Dobermans, Benjy and Speed Wizard, aka Weird.*

son, scolded that person, gave instructions, plotted and strategized with his advisors, just as the lord of the manor might have
done.

IN LATE 1971 we moved to Washington, D.C. *Rolling Stone*
sent Hunter to cover the 1972 presidential campaign. His articles were later published in book form as *Fear and Loathing on
the Campaign Trail '72*. Since he had to be in Washington for a
solid year, he decided to move us out there with him. I saw very
little of him that year. He traveled most of the time, following
George McGovern's campaign. When he was home, he was visiting friends, writing, or sleeping. I don't even remember seeing
him for a late afternoon breakfast or for the evening news.

We left Owl Farm in the care of two friends. Hunter drove his
Volvo 164 with a trailer full of stuff while Sandy and I flew to D.C.
to meet him. In November of 1971 we moved into a rented and furnished three-story redbrick house on a cul-de-sac on Juniper Street
in quiet, Northwest D.C., right on the edge of Rock Creek Park.
Rolling Stone magazine was paying for it; I can't imagine Hunter
selecting such a house otherwise. It was the sort of place for a doctor or a stockbroker. Redbrick with white trim around the windows, and a black, colonial-style lamppost at the end of the walk.
There was a huge, dark living room with a huge, dark, oak dining
table, a giant backyard with big trees, and an attached garage.
Over the garage, accessible through a door off the main stairway,
was a large office where Hunter worked. He called it the Fear
Room.

It's hard to convey the shock of moving from a funky ranch
house in the country outside Aspen to a colonial on the East

Coast. There was a garage-door opener; Owl Farm didn't even have a garage. This house had three stories, not including the basement; Owl Farm had one. The newspaper was thrown on our lawn each morning; in Woody Creek we had to drive about two miles to the Lenado Road turnoff to pick it up from our

In the Fear Room with Hunter at our house in Washington, D.C., while he was working on Fear and Loathing on the Campaign Trail '72. *His tools of the trade are all visible: beer, tape recorder, IBM Selectric,* The New York Times, *telephone, television, and cigarettes.*

newspaper box. Finally, it had Rock Creek Park right across the street.

The park was a wilderness in a very East Coast way—a uniform covering of bushy deciduous trees over a thick carpet of brush, and through the middle of the park ran the Rock Creek. I spent a lot of time roaming around the park either alone or with a friend, just exploring. It was the first time I had spent any time in the East, and the experience of wilderness was so completely different, just like everything that year. However, what stands out most for me was my school.

It's important to understand the division of labor between my mother and father, keeping in mind that they were, for all their disregard of some social conventions, children raised in the 1930s, '40s, and '50s in very conventional households. Hunter was the breadwinner, and Sandy was the housewife. As such, she was responsible for pretty much all aspects of raising me, including education. She was also responsible for tracking the finances, taking care of Hunter, and handling all the administrative aspects of a writer's life. She was interested in alternative education, "progressive education," as it was called then. There were no public charter schools in those days. Instead, some parents in Aspen, with the backing of George Stranahan, who was very interested in education, started something called the Aspen Community School. They brought in a teacher and educational philosopher from New Zealand named Sylvia Ashton-Warner, who had some strong opinions for the time that children should be engaged by teachers, rather than simply force-fed facts, and should be taught something more than blind obedience. I was a test subject. Over the years I bounced back and forth between the Aspen public schools and the Aspen Community School several times. I spent kindergarten and first grade at the public elementary school, and then moved to this experimental school for second grade. It was initially housed in the brand-new buildings of the Aspen Center for Physics, sponsored by the Aspen Institute, a now-famous think tank that was largely responsible for Aspen's cosmopolitan influence and perhaps its rapid commercialization and growth, and is also home to the Aspen Music Festival, the Design Conference, and countless other cultural/academic events. The whole complex was on the edge of town on a plateau that overlooked the Roaring Fork River. Behind the school was a giant field covered with tall native grasses. In front, there was a thick green lawn with a tiny stream running through it where, during lunchtime, we would have boat races with little pieces of wood in the fall and spring. At this school it was completely acceptable to wear a white T-shirt with a red circle on the front, and in the circle, in white script, the word "Cocaine" (instead of "Coca-Cola").

Pat Caddell, George McGovern, and Hunter on the 1972 campaign trail

When we moved to Washington, Sandy enrolled me in a nearby public elementary school. It was no such thing. It was a prison. The classes were large and the discipline strict. The building was huge and old. I remember long hallways with very high ceilings, the walls either beige or light green, and many doors down each side, off into the distance. The playground was fenced in, all asphalt. The rooms were cavernous, with many rows of desks. All it needed was a bunch of nuns to make it the polar opposite of what I had just come from. I hated it on sight and on principle and within a couple of days Sandy pulled me out.

But where to put me? She chose an experimental school called the Free School. It was operated out of a run-down, walk-up, second-story apartment in a grimy neighborhood of Washington. There were maybe ten other kids and between two and four teachers who were mostly young hippies with long hair, round John Lennon glasses, and big ideas about progressive education. The back window overlooked an alley full of trash. It was simply day care with a fancy name. I don't remember doing anything like traditional schoolwork the entire year, not that I objected. I had a great time. We either ran wild in the apartment or went on field trips, stuffed into the far back of a couple of VW Beetles. We went to the Smithsonian many times, and to the Washington Monument. Once we drove to New York City for a few days and slept on the floor of a school gym, visiting various landmarks by day. I remember climbing the stairs of the Statue of Liberty, reaching the top, and looking out the little windows in her crown at the skyline of New York. Some days we made candles by melting wax in pots on the kitchen stove and pouring them into molds. One day we broke a three-foot hole in the drywall between a room and the hallway. I don't remember being reprimanded or scolded.

When I talked to my mother about that school much later she said she had chosen it because a member of the Chicago Seven had sent his kid there. She said she did worry about the math curriculum, but that since I was already a competent and voracious reader, she figured I would be fine.

It was madness, of course. As a parent now, I wouldn't for a second consider putting my seven-year-old son in the hands of those well-meaning amateurs, doing nothing resembling schoolwork and spending the days in a tenement house in urban Washington, D.C. But I didn't come to any harm, and at the time it must have seemed like a good idea. If Hunter had an opinion about it, and in retrospect I'm sure he did, I never heard about it, we never talked about it, and I remained at the Free School for the remainder of that year. (I did end up repeating third grade, though, when I returned to Aspen, probably because there was no evidence I had done any schoolwork the previous year.)

The year in Washington ended with my mother's final pregnancy. She had been pregnant much of the time we were in Washington, but I was completely oblivious to it, except for one day when we had to get rid of our new cat, Ralph. We had gotten him when we came to Washington. I had always wanted a cat but I think Hunter felt the odds were heavily against a cat at Owl Farm because of the hawks, coyotes, bobcats, and other predators of small animals. One day Sandy told me that there was a disease in cat feces that could harm her baby, so we had to get rid of him. That was the first and last that I remember of any pregnancy. I think if she had shown up one day with a newborn, I would have been flabbergasted by the sudden appearance of a new member of the family. One day she went to the hospital and was there for a few days. When she came back there was no baby. Years later I learned it was a girl, and that she survived for a day

With Hunter in the kitchen at Owl Farm circa 1971,
when I was six, clowning around for the photographer

or so after being born. That was the last attempt at children for
my parents. Now I wonder how our lives would have been if I
had had a sibling; I would have been the older brother, protector,
and, perhaps, caregiver. We would have shared both the attention
and the fear.

We returned to Owl Farm from Washington following that
summer. I remember a huge Allied Van Lines truck in front of
our Washington house loading up boxes. I remember driving out
to Dulles International Airport with Sandy and riding on the
little elevated buses out to the airplane while Hunter drove the
car home to Woody Creek, to Owl Farm, to our sanctuary in
the high mountains of Colorado where we had friends, and space,
and the quiet of the country. I know we all were glad to be home,

where we could become again the happy, picturesque, offbeat, counterculture family we had been.

Unfortunately, it would be something very different. The offbeat family façade was crumbling, and I was old enough to see it happening. The next four years would be the worst of my life.

Uncle Ralph (Steadman) preparing to crush my skull with a rock in 1972 while we stand in Woody Creek, across the meadow from Owl Farm

THREE

Awakening: ages 10 to 13

*A young horseman and his lamb—Building fires, hauling
firewood—Trouble with guns—I was a teenage hit man—
The Beating—My fear, bitterness, and shame*

HST TIMELINE

1974   Travels to Kinshasa, Zaire, to cover the Muhammad Ali–George
Foreman Heavyweight Championship fight.
Hunter and Jann Wenner organize the Elko conference,
intended to lay out a platform and strategy to use the Youth
Vote to take control of national politics.
Starts doing university lectures.
Considers running for Colorado senate.

1975   Travels to Saigon, South Vietnam, to cover the fall of that city
to the Viet Cong.

WHEN I WAS AROUND ten years old, I began to look
up from the ground at my feet to see the world around
me. I began to notice other people as real and separate beings. Up
until then, my friends' parents were not people, they were just
parents. Once they were out of sight, they ceased to exist. The

same was true of my own parents. I had no awareness that my mother had a life, or feelings, or interests, beyond me.

It was also a time of disillusionment. My parents' marriage was gradually falling apart, and though I was not consciously aware of this, it affected me. I felt better when I was around parents who liked each other. I also began to suspect that my father's anger was not always just and fair. Up until then there had been no questioning it: if my father was angry, I was wrong. As I raised my eyes up, I began to suspect that justice wasn't always the governing principle of his rage.

This happened gradually, in the background, amid school, friends, chores, lots and lots of books, building fires in the fireplace, model rockets, my first gun, horseback riding, my first record player, and my first motorcycle.

I remember building fires. My father was a purist when it came to fires. We had a giant fireplace in the living room that we kept burning most nights in the winter. Cords and cords of split spruce and piñon logs were stacked up against the sides of the house in the fall. I would gather wood from these stacks in the winter. My father insisted a fire couldn't be started by artificial means; it had to be done authentically. He patiently showed me the process: first a base of crumpled-up newspaper, then kindling, then small fast-burning logs of spruce on top of the kindling, and once they were burning well, the big, dense logs of piñon that needed a lot of heat to catch fire and then burned for hours. And then start everything with a single match. No lighter fluid, no combustible fire logs, just a match. I mastered the purist method and later, whenever I came to visit, right up until the day he died, and it was cold enough for a fire, Hunter would ask me to start one. I would gladly comply. We both understood that this was my job and I was good at it, and it made me happy that he asked.

As a child of ten or so, before building the fire, I first had to go down into the basement to gather kindling. I was afraid of the basement, especially at night. I would go down the stairs with a flashlight and into the cavernous area where the kindling was, gather as much as I could into the canvas tote, and then run back upstairs as fast as I could, imagining the claws and teeth of some demon just behind me. I would get to the top of the stairs where I could look into the bright kitchen then turn and look back down the stairs, out of breath from fear rather than exertion. There was nothing, of course, but that didn't prevent me from imagining those claws each time I looked down into the black maw of the basement stairwell.

If the log supply was low, I had to go outside. I'd dress for winter and take my flashlight and the canvas tote through the deep snow to collect first the spruce, then the piñon logs. Unlike the basement, the darkness of the winter night was comforting, like a thick down jacket. The night sky outside of Aspen is a canopy of what seems like an infinite number of hard little points of light that shine steadily rather than twinkle, and in which the vague ribbon of the Milky Way can be easily discerned stretching from one horizon to the other.

Being small and the logs large and heavy, I usually had to make several trips, but I didn't mind. I was at home, in my valley with my mountains, my sky, my stars, my deep winter night, and it comforted me. I think Hunter must have felt this way also, standing alone on the porch or in front of the giant picture windows of the living room late at night or perhaps at dawn when everyone else was asleep. It was our home, an anchor, not just a house, but a place and a feeling of deep-rootedness. It was always a place of comfort to return to, in spite of everything that happened inside that house, even long after I moved out, even now.

He must have felt proud. He had written three books that would become classics: *Hell's Angels, Fear and Loathing in Las Vegas,* and *Fear and Loathing on the Campaign Trail '72.* He had become a well-known journalist. In 1975 *Rolling Stone* sent him to Saigon in Vietnam, his first stint as a Gonzo war correspondent. He owned a house on 140 acres of land in the Colorado mountains, the nearest neighbors were at least a half mile away and out of sight, and he had good friends and a family. For a moment, perhaps, he may have felt that his life was what he had hoped it would be, that he was successful in spite of all the struggles, self-imposed and otherwise.

Meanwhile, I went about my childhood. In the summer especially I spent most of my time outside, either alone or with friends. But summertime for an only child in the country could

The Elko conference in 1974, with Hunter's notes

be challenging. I liked to be alone and had many diversions such as reading, inventing games, building and launching model rockets, and target shooting with my BB gun, but there was a limit to how much solitude I could bear. I would see my friends now and then, but that required coordination and transportation. One summer, in an effort to keep me occupied, Sandy took me down to a small riding stable a couple of miles from home that taught horseback riding.

The outfit consisted of a small riding ring, a stable painted yellow and peeling, four or five horses, a hay barn, a tiny office, and a tack shed. The instructor's name was Cecily. Sandy signed me up for lessons and I got started. Cecily had defined a hierarchy of experience levels. Each level required a certain number of hours of instruction on horseback, book study, and a test. When a student completed a level successfully, they got a gold star on a grid on the wall indicating their level. Being a sucker for this kind of achievement, I started in and quickly reached the first two levels. However, each level required time and therefore money, and it became clear that my parents could not afford to pay for as much instruction time as I wanted. So we worked out a deal: I worked at the stables in return for free riding lessons and riding time. It became my first summer job.

Each morning I would ride my Kawasaki 90 motorcycle down to the stables, maybe three miles from home, and feed the horses. This consisted of opening a bale of hay and heaving a heavy slice of the bale for each horse over the paddock fence. While they were eating the hay, I would muck the stables, which means I would shovel the horseshit out of each stable into a wheelbarrow and dump it on a huge pile in the back. As I became more proficient at riding I would help teach the newcomers and later even take tourists on guided horseback rides around Woody Creek.

I spent my days there with Cecily, her boyfriend, Jan, and the other student employee, a girl named Amy Erickson, on whom I quickly developed a powerful crush. In addition to riding classes, Cecily organized picnics and overnights for the students. The best spot was a mile or two from the stables down by the Roaring Fork River. There was a small field of deep green grass right by the river, surrounded by cottonwoods and aspens. The river had carved a deep trench by the near bank, which made an excellent swimming hole, and a rope dangled from an overhanging tree. We picnicked several times there that summer and the next and once camped by the river, hobbling our horses and letting them graze among the rich grass while we slept. Amy and I became good friends, and though she didn't return my affections, one morning after camping out she told me that she had awoken early in the morning to find that we were holding hands through our sleeping bags. I thought that was wonderfully romantic.

Cecily also had riding competitions and trucked us to nearby fairs and 4-H shows so Amy and I could compete in the riding events such as Western Showmanship, Western Pleasure, and the 4-H Gymkhana. Amy and I would pretty up our horses the evening before with shampoo and conditioner, comb their manes and tails, and wash and polish our tack (saddles and bridles). The next morning we dressed up in our cowboy hats, western shirts, jeans, and boots. Amy was a better rider than I was, but I won a few blue ribbons that summer also, which I displayed on my bedroom bookshelf. Cecily was proud of us both and never encouraged any kind of competition between us.

The next summer Cecily enrolled Amy and me in a 4-H program to raise and show sheep. She made a deal with us: she would buy two lambs and pay for their food, vet bills, and any other expenses if we agreed to care for, train, and show them at the 4-H show at the end of that summer. She was entitled to any money won in competition. We agreed, and promptly became the guardians of two lambs, Sunny and Sammy. That summer when we weren't riding, Amy and I were training our lambs to stand in the proper sheep stance with their rear legs back, backs straight, and heads up and still, or to follow at our heels as we walked in a circle, then stop on command. It took all summer because they weren't the quickest learners, but constant repetition paid off. We showed them at the local 4-H Fair, where Sunny won Reserve Grand Champion and was bought for four hundred dollars. Though I was a country boy, I wasn't a farm boy. Years later I realized that the man who bought Sunny probably didn't buy her because he wanted a pet lamb. I just hope her end was quick and painless.

The stable became my little family for those two summers. Cecily's boyfriend, Jan, was a kind, thoughtful guy who took an interest in me, and we became friends and continued to write to each other even after he and Cecily had broken up. I was in boarding school by then, and he was living on Long Island. Cecily was a laid-back mother figure, maintaining order with a gentle hand, never losing her temper, easily managing a small swarm of children, teaching us horsemanship and having fun at the same time.

My parents knew almost nothing about how I spent my days those two summers, though I learned much later that Hunter knew of and approved of my work at the stables. Though I told Sandy about the horse shows and my sheep Sunny, neither she nor Hunter ever came to any of the shows nor ever came to the stables after that first day. I don't recall Amy's parents ever attending our horse shows either. As a parent I am very conscientious about acknowledging my son's tiniest achievements and attending all his events, but perhaps my son will complain in the years to come that we shouldn't have made such a big deal about every little thing.

Hunter was traveling quite a bit. He had begun to do university lectures and in 1974 went to Zaire with Ralph Steadman to cover the famous Ali-Foreman Heavyweight Championship fight for *Rolling Stone* (one of many assignments he never did complete). Not that this meant anything to me at the time. All I knew is that for a few weeks, it was much calmer at home, and then suddenly one day Hunter reappeared bearing gifts for Sandy and me. From Zaire, he brought me a pair of souvenir gold boxing gloves that are still hanging on the living room wall at Owl Farm. Sometime shortly afterward, two giant elephant tusks appeared on the mantel over the fireplace, smuggled into the country god knows how.

In general, Hunter wasn't one to acknowledge holidays or special days. My mother organized my birthday parties and I don't remember him ever being a part of them. Every now and then, though, he would do something significant. One Christmas he bought me a combination record player/tuner/amplifier with separate speakers. I remember him carrying this big box through the front door one night and saying it was for me. I promptly set it up in my bedroom, grabbed a few records from Hunter's collection, and began playing a record every night as I went to sleep, singing along with the songs. I cycled through a small selection of records including Jimmy Buffett's early albums and the Grateful Dead's *Workingman's Dead.* I can still sing most of those songs from memory.

I see now that the boxing gloves and the stereo were awkward tokens of love. Hunter wasn't much for demonstrations of love, at least not his love of family and friends (lovers were an entirely different matter), so he did it through gifts. For Hunter, the gloves represented Ali and his victory, and Ali was one of the few people Hunter unabashedly admired with the enthusiasm of a fan. Ali was extremely smart, funny, courageous, and good with words, all qualities Hunter admired. It didn't hurt that they both grew up in Louisville, Kentucky. Ali won the fight against Foreman not through strength but through strategy, something that deeply impressed Hunter. The gloves weren't just souvenirs, they were symbols of the victory of intelligence and chutzpah over brute strength, and I think he gave these to me as some kind of talisman. It would have helped if he had tried to explain this to me at the time, since I cared about boxing about as much as I cared about the GDP of small central African nations and knew nothing about Ali or the fight, but better late than never.

It was the same with the record player. Music was extremely important to Hunter—if the TV wasn't showing a football game or the network news, music was always playing. Back in the 1970s he had a sound engineer build him a set of speakers audacious in their conception. They consisted of eight separate enclosures containing a total of eighty separate speakers. Each woofer box had four sixteen-inch cones, and each tweeter-midrange box had sixteen little speakers in a tall, narrow cabinet. These pairs of enclosures stood like four monoliths in each corner of the living room, were loud as hell, and were Hunter's pride for many years. Later, he bought a Nakamichi mobile sound system that included a high-end cassette player and two small but very heavily powered speakers that fit into a dark gray plastic suitcase that, when loaded, weighed around thirty pounds. I can only imagine how he terrorized his neighbors in hotels as he traveled around the country, cranking up Jefferson Airplane's "White Rabbit" at three a.m. I'm sure he wanted to pass on his love of music to me, as I hope to pass it on to my son. It would be many years, though, until I could appreciate his gifts and his motives.

I was coming to fear him more and respect him less. His anger, quick to erupt and unpredictable, was a terrifying thing, and could be triggered by trivial provocations. It seemed that when I did get his attention, it was more likely to take the form of an angry outburst about something I had done wrong.

As an only child and a curious one who wanted to know how things worked, I often took things apart. I didn't always know how to put them back together so they worked again. Often this was harmless because the subject of my investigations was a toy of mine or something from the secondhand store, but sometimes I would investigate machines that were still useful, like Hunter's portable cassette recorders. When I failed to make them work again, Hunter would yell something like: "You stupid waterhead bastard! What the fuck have you done! If you've broken this, goddammit, I'll give you a beating you'll never forget!" The fact that he had never beaten me before did not stop me from being absolutely certain that he would this time. I almost always got the machines to work again, and he never did beat me, but I couldn't forget my fear of him. I couldn't understand at the time that this was just bluster and noise. I was terrified of him. Just because he didn't beat me this time didn't mean he wouldn't beat me next time.

There was one time when we were living in Washington, D.C., that I still remember clearly. It must have been shortly after we moved there. I was playing with the remote garage-door opener, a new and fascinating toy for me. I somehow locked it inside an antique bureau that came with the house, and I had no idea how to open it again. When I realized what I had done and that I could not undo it, I was absolutely terrified. What would happen when Hunter found out? I must have told Sandy, though I can't remember what she told me. Whatever it was must not have been comforting because I went up to my room and hid under my bed. I was sure that when Hunter returned, he was going to beat me. I don't know what I was thinking. That he wouldn't find me? He wouldn't see me under the tall, narrow bed? And what if he didn't see me? Did I think he would go about his night as if there were nothing strange about his seven-year-old son being missing from the house?

It was a long wait. I lay under the bed imagining the worst: how he would enter my room huge and terrible like a giant warrior from a Viking legend, his eyes small and vicious, his walk and all his movements radiating dangerous power and rage. Then the yelling and cursing, "You stupid waterhead freak!" and so on, one colorful and poisonous curse after another—followed finally by the inevitable and unavoidable punishment—a beating. Fully appreciating the power of the right word, he never called it a spanking or even a whipping. He always called it a Beating, with its implication of severe pain. A Beating implies the overwhelming physical dominance of one person over another, with no mercy and no restraint, in which the victim is bloody, broken, utterly vanquished, and pathetic. I was sure my beating would involve a belt, though he had never used a belt before, and that he would hit me very hard, many times. I didn't think about exactly how many times he would hit me, or where. All I knew for sure is that it would be excruciatingly painful.

With this scene of horror in my mind, I hid like a dog that had crapped on the rug, trembling, in the smallest, farthest corner it could find, waiting for the boot to the ribs and the heavy stick on the back.

He never came. There was no Beating. In fact, he never beat me, not so much as a spanking, a whipping, or even a slap. I remember him and Sandy trying to reach the landlord to find out where the key to the bureau was, and then later that evening a locksmith coming to unlock the drawer. Beyond that, nothing— no reprimand, nothing. Maybe I was wrong about him.

Or maybe there were worse things than beatings. One day I got my hands on a pellet gun of Hunter's and was trying it out. I had had a Daisy spring-loaded BB gun rifle for years as well as a spring-loaded .45 replica that spit out a BB about fifteen feet on a good day. In contrast, Hunter's CO_2-powered pellet gun was powerful—definitely worth playing with. Somehow I managed to jam the tiny lead pellet in the breech, and in the stupidity of panic, dreading the consequences, I didn't confess but put the gun away and hoped he wouldn't find out. Of course he did—it was just a matter of time—and he was furious. This time, though, he didn't rage and then let it pass. This time he was furious in a new way. He didn't yell, he was cold and angry. There was no sign of forgiveness or understanding. He unscrewed the front sight from the pellet gun, gave it to me, and told me to carry it with me as a reminder of what I had done, of what a stupid thing I had done. And that was it. Of course I knew I had made a mistake, and had compounded it by trying to cover it up. Of course I felt horribly guilty about it. When he gave me that sight as a talisman of shame, though, I hated him for it. We never talked about it again, but I still resent him for it.

I look back on these incidents from my perspective of the

present and my own fatherhood, and I consider different ways of looking at them. I know from my own experience with my son that I would be angry also if I found a useful machine dismantled on the living room floor, or I found that he had broken something and hidden it away in fear and shame. I don't doubt that Hunter was trying to teach me responsibility through consequences, but I can't find a way to understand the cruelty, because it felt like more than punishment.

Then, there was the .410 shotgun incident, which he handled uncharacteristically well. On my tenth or eleventh birthday he had given me a small-bore .410 shotgun of my own, well suited to my size. This was my first real gun and also a serious, dangerous weapon. It was a rite of passage and an indication of his trust in me. He made one condition: I was not to kill any animals. I agreed, and for a year or so I would bring it out during clay pigeon shooting contests in the yard, a favorite pastime of Hunter's. Then one day I got the idea to try to shoot a magpie. I had nothing against them; I just wanted to see if I could actually hit one. I took my shotgun into the fields behind the house and took several shots at some birds, missing all of them. I gave up and returned to the house and laid the gun on the couch in the kitchen, intending to put it away. However, I got distracted and later that day Hunter noticed the gun on the couch. He asked what I had been doing with it, and if I had been shooting at birds. I admitted that I had. He picked up the gun and took it downstairs and put it with his own guns. He didn't yell, he didn't rage, he didn't call me names. He just took the gun back. I was sad and ashamed, but I was not angry at him. It was fair and just.

I had lost my first gun because I had violated the ban on killing animals. However, there was an exception—shooting gophers for hire. One summer when I was twelve I became a hit man for our neighbors. They had a serious gopher infestation in their lawn and they hired me to take care of it. I got permission from Hunter to use his 20-gauge shotgun to shoot the little bastards, and for a few weeks I would hike up the road to the mesa overlooking our house with the gun and a pocketful of shells, present myself at the neighbors' door, and after some juice and cookies, get to work. This meant sitting very still in a giant field of dirt and weeds with the shotgun loaded and pointed, waiting for a gopher to come up out of his hole and stand up. They are easily spooked and work together to protect the colony. When one gopher perceives danger he starts squeaking and then all the nearby gophers flee to their holes and dive. The trick was to not have to move much to get one in my sights. I was patient, I was determined, and I was paid per head, and I killed dozens that summer. I wonder what the neighbors thought of repeated shotgun blasts in the middle of a summer day, day after day, but no one complained. That was part of the beauty of growing up in the country. Guns were a part of life, and neighbors left each other alone unless there was a damn good reason to interfere.

My employers for the gopher extermination were Carol and Palmer, a young couple who rented the house on the mesa next to us for a few years. Carol was Mrs. Cleaver for the '70s. She was tall, slim, beautiful, and very kind to me. Her husband, Palmer, was a mellow guy from the South who smiled a lot, talked slowly, and had an accent that was easy on the ears. Going to their house was like coming in from the cold. It was bright, clean, and calm. There was no tension here, just peace. Seeking refuge, I spent more and more time with them that summer. I could no more imagine Palmer going into a rage than I could imagine him sprouting another pair of arms. The pot helped, no doubt, but then they were the Cleavers for the '70s, not the '50s. Being in their presence was a balm, particularly since by 1976 my parents' marriage was quickly disintegrating and they were no longer able to hide their conflicts, which were growing louder and more savage.

With Hunter and Sandy circa 1977, when I
was thirteen, just before their separation and
divorce. We were not a happy family.

FOUR

The Breakup

"He who makes a beast of himself gets rid of the pain of being a man."—Broken glass in the morning—Victim, witness, judge—In the Bahamas with Buffett—California, the Promised Land—Police in the night—Leaving for the last time

HST TIMELINE

1976   '76 presidential campaign.
        Hears Jimmy Carter's Law Day speech and endorses him for president.
        Coverage of Jimmy Carter in *Rolling Stone* magazine.

1977   Continues to lecture at college campuses for next several years.

S OMEWHERE AROUND 1976, when I was twelve, the conflicts between Hunter and Sandy reached new and frightening levels, and I came to despise my father. It was the fighting that did it. Looking back, my mother and father had probably been fighting for years, but I didn't know that at the time. I suppose I knew that parents fought, but I had never seen my own parents fight. Up until then, they had managed to keep their voices down to avoid waking me. Finally, though, their fights escalated into outright war in the middle of the night with shouting, crying, things being thrown and broken, and eventually the arrival of the police.

As I recollect today, I am struck by the absence of any connection between the late-night fights and my daytime world. The fighting took place in an alternate universe that came into being in the middle of the night and was gone the next morning. I went to school, I played with my friends, I read Hardy Boys books and Archie comics, built model cars and eighteen-wheelers, cleaned my room and mowed the half-acre lawn, and I never talked about what was happening at night to anyone. It wasn't a conscious effort to hide anything; it was as if those terrible fights were utterly detached from my real life. It was a little bubble of a recurring nightmare that held only my mother, my father, and me.

The first time I entered that bubble I woke from a deep sleep, not knowing why I was awake, and heard the shouting. At first I didn't know what was happening, or who was screaming. And then I realized it was my mother, and that the deeper voice yelling was my father. I don't know which was worse, waking up and not knowing what was happening, or waking up to realize that it was my parents. There were brief intervals of silence when I couldn't hear their voices, and then out of the silence came Hunter's voice, sharp and powerful, followed by my mother's voice, high and shrill. Then there would be silence or murmuring, then more yelling and shouting. There I was, willing myself not to wake up fully, hidden in the dark, wishing that I could just go back to sleep and pretend this wasn't happening. Hunter was not simply angry, he was enraged. My mother wasn't just frustrated, she was furious and terrified. Each was trying to overpower the other. It went on and on. Their fear and rage rolled through my dark room like huge ocean waves. I just wanted it to stop.

The next morning the memory would fade like an evil dream. And then, days or weeks later, it would happen again, I would be dragged out of sleep in the middle of the night and I would again try to forget, try to find that safe and comfortable place where parents didn't fight.

This went on for months. Each time when I woke I felt a shock like cold electricity, and I clenched up inside. The battles got longer and louder. Some nights there was a new sound, the smash of glass or ceramic shattering like a bomb. Eventually I would fall asleep again—I can't imagine how.

The next morning I would look for evidence of what had been broken. Usually my mother would clean up the mess before I woke, but not always. I remember one morning finding the remains of a watermelon spread across the kitchen and into the living room. Often it was plates of food or glasses. I remember worrying about what had been lost. Was it something important, something sentimental? One time it was a pottery plate that Hunter had brought back from Mexico or South America before I was born, and that had hung over the kitchen sink for as long as I could remember. It was as if each of those objects was a physical manifestation of our family, that they represented the good memories and were the glue that held us together.

I think it was only Hunter who threw things. It may be that Sandy threw things also, though even now I recoil inside at the thought. Certainly my mother wouldn't do such a thing to our family. And throwing something at Hunter with the intention of hurting him, or to intentionally break something important to him, would be like jabbing a rabid grizzly bear with a spear. His retaliation would be massive and without mercy.

One night, while I lay awake, waiting for the screaming to stop, there came again the crash of something smashing against the floor or the wall. This time it was too much. I jumped out of bed and walked out into the kitchen, hoping that the sight of me would make them stop.

It worked. They saw me and stopped shouting, looked away in embarrassment, and told me not to worry and to go back to bed. I did, and there was no more fighting that night.

There were other fights, of course. For a while I found that by getting out of bed and walking into the kitchen, I could make them stop. Eventually, this approach no longer worked. I would make my appearance, they would stop, I would go back to sleep, and then they would begin flogging each other again. Finally, one night I walked out into the kitchen and waited for them to stop, and they just kept fighting.

I couldn't let this continue. I thought that perhaps I could help sort things out for them. I listened for a while to Sandy, and I listened to Hunter's responses. If I understood the issue, I thought, surely I could help them come to an understanding, and they would calm down so our world would stop shaking. But Sandy was crying, always crying, and sometimes screaming in frustrated rage. Sometimes I could barely understand her words because she was screaming or sobbing. Hunter was angry too, but even when he was roaring, he was angry in a controlled and directed way. They were like two boxers, one calm and experienced, the other wild, exhausted, flailing in undisciplined rage and desperation. The difference was that Hunter used words, not his fists, as his weapons. Whatever Sandy said, Hunter would take those words and twist them. She would become angrier, more frustrated, and more unhinged.

It was clear to me that the antidote to this craziness was reason, calm, and some mediation. They would smile and kiss, and all would be well again in our home. My mother needed an advocate, someone who could calmly defend her and get my father to listen. She took care of me every day, bought my clothes, fed me, drove me to see my friends, and tucked me in at night. At the time, it seemed right and necessary that I should step up and be that advocate. I spoke in my quiet twelve-year-old voice, and tried to explain to Hunter what Sandy had just said, and suggested that they calm down.

I had no effect. They went right on with the death match, my mother doomed every time to humiliating failure. I tried a few more times to introduce reason and was consistently ignored. I began to realize that Hunter was interested in winning, not understanding.

I began to suspect that his misunderstanding was intentional, more than that—malicious. He was trying to break her down. He didn't care what she was trying to say, he cared about breaking her. And that's what he did. With a combination of deliberate distortions and carefully chosen words that would inflict maximum hurt, along with his deep and powerful voice, he crushed her, over and over again, until she understood that he was the master, that he was in control.

As I watched these fights, I began to understand these things about my father on a gut level. Whereas earlier I saw a lack of communication, I began to see a deliberate intent to harm, and that was when I began to hate my father. I saw him bullying, provoking, and insulting my mother. Before, I had assumed my father broke things in a thoughtless rage, but now I began to suspect that he broke things that were important to Sandy to inflict greater pain. He was in a fury, yes, but I began to believe that there was a vein of deliberate cruelty running through his rage.

Sometimes I would be especially angered by something he said, and I would speak up to defend my mother. Thankfully, he ignored me. Had he turned his full rage and malice on me then, I am sure I would have been incinerated like a soldier before a flamethrower.

Finally, one night, my mother invited the outside world in. She did the unthinkable and called the state patrol. Two troopers showed up within minutes and they looked profoundly nervous, no doubt having heard all kinds of rumors about the dangerous, anarchic, heavily armed drug fiend and his gun collection. This legendary fiend greeted them calmly at the door, shook hands with them, and apologized for their having to come out to a scene like this. He was relaxed, smiling, and charming. He intimated that Sandy was drunk, that they had had a disagreement, like married couples do, and she had become hysterical and called the police. Their relief was obvious. They would not have to try to arrest this man, there would be no showdown with guns. This was a simple domestic incident between a calm and reasonable man and his drunken wife.

One of the officers spoke to my mother. Sandy was crying, and mumbled and sobbed something about what he had done, only a few words of which they could understand. Hunter continued his good-old-boy routine, and after fifteen or twenty minutes they left. They had done nothing to help her. She had invoked the plan of last resort and it had no effect. He made it clear to her that she was utterly helpless. I was outraged; he was a monster, a bastard, and a dangerous man.

What is so remarkable now, as I look back, is that she very likely *was* drunk, and so was he. Hunter had been drinking heavily and consistently since he was a teenager, and by the mid-'70s my mother was drinking heavily as well. In retrospect, it would be naïve to think that those vicious fights did not proceed directly from a long night of boozing and the ingestion of who knows what that stripped away all self-control and perspective. But this did not occur to a twelve-year-old at the time, and I was incensed that he was telling the police my mother was a drunk. It never occurred to me that had they been sober, those terrible fights might never have taken place. But based on what I knew and understood then, it was crystal clear to me that my father was a beast, and my mother his victim.

The only thing that changed after that night with the police was that my mother, without Hunter's knowledge, began ses-

With Hunter and Sandy in the kitchen at Owl Farm in the late 1970s. By this time the kitchen got an upgrade to butcher-block countertops, some tile, and a new stove.

sions with a Gestalt therapist. She told me his name was Stewart. They met once a week and she seemed happier after their meetings. She and my father still fought constantly, and when a fight became a pitched battle in the middle of the night, I still got up and watched. I was no longer interested in mediating because it was clear my father was not interested in the facts; I was now gathering evidence against him, and those fights provided plenty of it.

In the midst of this foul craziness, Hunter announced one day in the fall of 1977 that I was going sailing in the Bahamas with Jimmy Buffett, at the time a little-known musician with a few radio hits. I was to be a member of the crew—the cabin boy, I was told. It was to be for about a month, there would be other guests coming and going from the boat, and Jane, Jimmy's fiancée at the time, would be with us. I was thrilled. I had been a fan of Buffett for a couple of years and had learned by heart all the songs on his first couple of albums. I had also been taking sailing classes at a reservoir near Aspen, and the idea of being able to sail on a real sailboat on the ocean was irresistible.

Looking back, it seems very strange that my parents would have agreed to take me out of school and send me off to spend a month on a sailboat in the Bahamas with a bunch of strangers and a guy who already had a reputation as a man who liked to party. It turned out Hunter had asked Jimmy to take me sailing. While working on this book I asked Jimmy how that trip came about. He said Hunter was worried about me. Hunter was concerned about the effect of the divorce on me, and thought that some time away from Aspen would be good for me. "I always thought it was out of a true sense of love that he made that decision to send you sailing with me," he told me.

More broadly, Jimmy said Hunter was very concerned about

*Hunter and Jimmy Buffett in Buffett's apartment
in Key West, where Hunter spent several months*

the effect his lifestyle had on me. He said, "Like all of us back then, we were not that equipped to be responsible parents and I think that bothered him. It bothered me. I guess in a way we wanted to raise you to pearls, not oysters, but I believe were mistaken in the belief that how we lived our lives would work for our kids.

"Hunter was always concerned about your well-being," he said, "and admitted on several occasions to me that he felt guilty about how he lived his life, and how it might affect you. I think that was the reason he asked me to take you sailing. . . . I think he was very happy that you and I developed a bond, I think that was what he was hoping for, as he might have seen me as less crazy than him and some kind of a better influence that he was able to produce." When I asked him how I saw my relationship with Hunter change over the years, he said, "As you got older, I truly believe you were an anchor for him. As his world seemed to get crazier the older he got, he really cherished you."

I didn't know any of this at the time, though I wish I had. I just knew I was going sailing in the Bahamas with my favorite musician. And, just as important, I could escape the dreadful tension at home that was becoming increasingly more oppressive. I flew down to Miami by myself and met Jimmy and Jane. We spent a week or so there while the work on Buffet's new thirty-three-foot fiberglass-hulled ketch, *Euphoria,* was being completed. He was having all manner of customizations added to it—ratlines, lots of teak, and old-fashioned port/starboard brass lamps. I hung out on the boat, running errands with the carpenters, doing whatever odd jobs needed to be done. I remember the omnipresent smell of powerful weed. I also remember one evening sitting at the top of the ladder leading down into the cabin while several adults gathered around the galley table talking and listening to James Taylor's latest album. Suddenly a lot of white powder went spraying across the table onto the floor, and two or three agitated adults were immediately on their knees trying to gather all that powder back together.

Once the boat work was complete, we set sail for Bimini, just east of Miami across the Gulf Stream. I remember midway across, in the midst of a storm that drove Miss Jane and me belowdecks to wait out our seasickness, Jimmy suddenly yelled for help. I popped my head up and saw the bow of a giant freighter like a black wall looming up over us out of the pouring rain. In his haste to get on deck, P. J. O'Rourke, a young journalist at the time, staggered out of the tiny bathroom and lurched for the ladder to the deck, one hand holding his pants, which were still hanging around his knees. The freighter narrowly missed us, and we made it safely to the port of Alice Town in the Bimini Islands, where Hemingway had spent some time, according to a plaque in the local bar.

We sailed leisurely south along the string of tiny islands that make up the Bahamas, anchoring each night off the shore of some nameless hillock of an island with a deserted white sand beach and crowned by a tuft of pale green vegetation. The sky was clear and the water was warm, and we often jumped off the boat in the mornings or evenings to swim and cool off. Sometimes we stopped at a small town for groceries, conch fritters, and for the adults a cold beer at the local bar. We stopped for a few days in Nassau and finally reached Great Exuma Island where I disembarked for the flight home to Colorado.

Various friends of Jimmy's came and went during the trip. I was crew and cabin boy, and on safe stretches I would take the helm and hold a compass heading as though our lives depended on it. I was determined to be a good helmsman to validate Jimmy's trust in me, and I focused my whole being on holding the boat to the course. I can still see clearly the large compass dial with its white digits on a black background mounted just in front of the wheel and the dim red light that illuminated it during night cruises.

Jimmy taught me how to read charts and how to plot our position using a bearing compass and dead reckoning. He began to teach me to use the sextant to determine our position from the angle of the sun, but that was a tricky art that I did not master before the end of the journey. I learned how to properly tie off a line on a cleat, how to use the winches, how to set the anchor, and how much slack to leave in the chain. I learned how to lower the sails and fold them so that they would unfurl neatly when raised again. I became captain of the Zodiac rubber dinghy that we towed behind us, and I was light enough that I could get it to plane on the water when I cranked open the throttle of its small Mercury outboard motor. I also learned how to scrub teak, polish brass, coil line, and do other lowly tasks suitable for a cabin boy. And I loved it. This wasn't work, this was an apprenticeship, and I wanted to master it.

At one point we were staying at Staniel Cay for a few days, and I wanted a sweatshirt that had the Staniel Cay Yacht Club logo printed on it. I had not come on this trip with any money, so I asked Jimmy if he could buy it for me. He agreed, but in return he told me I would have to scrub the icebox on the boat. It was a deal. The next day I crawled down into the icebox, just a big insulated box under the cockpit seats large enough for a thirteen-year-old boy to crouch in, and spent a couple of hours in the hot sun scrubbing the surfaces, draining the scum, and then restocking it with ice, then food. It was hard work, but I didn't mind it a bit. I considered myself lucky to earn that sweatshirt. More than that, I was eager to have chores and work. I wanted to learn to be a sailor, I wanted to earn my right to take the helm and determine our position. Jimmy was a patient teacher and he was happy to do it, and when circumstances called for it, as when we were nearly run down by that freighter, he was firm and knowledgeable.

It was an extraordinary trip. Jimmy was famously laid-back, we were in no hurry, the weather was calm, the whole pace of life in those tiny islands was slow and easy. Best of all, there was no fighting, no screaming, just a boatful of slow-moving, stoned, happy people. Except me, of course. No drugs for the cabin boy.

As I look back on that trip, though, what stands out most clearly is not the sailing and the water and the beaches, wonderful as that was, but the lack of tension and the surrogate fathering of Jimmy. For that time he filled a great need in me for the attention, care, and guidance of a man who gave me the opportunity to earn his trust and respect. I will always be grateful to him.

When I returned home the situation had not improved. I hadn't thought about it the whole time I was gone, except to appreciate the lack of tension, and I'm sure this is exactly what Hunter hoped for. Later that spring things finally came to a head. It happened during the day, when I wasn't home. What I know is from my mother, and her memories of that day are in turn filtered through more than thirty years and, like all memories, like my own memories, are shaped by what she wanted to remember.

She was in her room when Hunter came in, yelling at her about something. She looked up and told him, "Hunter, I'm going to get a divorce." She says he became furious, began searching the room for her journal writings, and when he found them he built a fire in the fireplace and started burning the pages, along with her photos. At that point Sandy called the sheriff's office to ask for help in leaving the house. The sheriff and his deputies were doing an all-day encounter workshop together (this was Aspen in the '70s, and the sheriff, Dick Keinast, had a degree in philosophy and theology), and there was only one deputy on duty. Shortly afterward the deputy, a young, soft-spoken man, who like all the deputies at the time did not carry a gun, came to the door. He asked, "Does he have any guns?" She told him that he did, that he had many, and that they were loaded. She says he was obviously frightened. Then Hunter came to the door and told him, as he had told police before, that he was sorry he had to come all this way, that his wife had been drinking again, and that there was no problem. He might as well leave. Meanwhile, the fire was still burning, and Hunter continued to put more of her papers and photos in the fireplace. Sandy told the deputy that Hunter was burning her things, and she says he told her, "I'm sorry, ma'am, there's nothing I can do." With the deputy watching, she got the car keys, got in our blue Datsun 510 wagon, probably only with her purse and the clothes she was wearing, and drove into Aspen to pick me up. She learned later that as soon as she left, Hunter piled most of her clothes in the driveway and set them on fire.

What strikes me now is that I used the pronoun "we" whenever I talked about that first separation. I said, "we left," or, "when we left Hunter," as if I helped to make the decision, as if Sandy and I were partners, rather than mother and son. Yet that's exactly how it felt, that we were a team united against my father. To me, he was a very bad man who tormented my mother, whom I loved dearly and depended upon.

I remember riding in the car to a little motel in downtown Aspen, where we checked in. I remember it was important that Hunter not be able to find us because we thought he might hurt us if he did. He had an extensive network of friends and acquaintances in Aspen, which was a very small community, and in retrospect, I'm sure he knew exactly where we were, or at least he knew that he could find us with a couple of phone calls, and that he chose to not contact us. At the time, though, I only knew he was furious and dangerous, and I was terrified of what he might do if he found us. We stayed at the motel for a couple of days, and then we packed up the Datsun and drove west to California, to stay with Betty Benton and her children for a couple of weeks at her house in Marin County, just north of San Francisco.

Tom and Betty Benton were my parents' best friends in the early and mid-'70s. Tom was a silk-screen artist, political activist, and Hunter's collaborator for many years on broadsheets, book covers, and campaign posters, as well as the iconic Gonzo fist and blade. They had a three-story cinder-block gallery/home in the middle of Aspen that Tom had built with his own hands in the late '60s. Tom's studio was on the top floor, the gallery was at the front of the building, and the rest of the building was living space for Tom, Betty, and their two children, Brian and Michelle. Brian was a year older than I, Michelle a year or two younger. Brian and I were good friends and tormented his sister and her friends whenever we could.

I loved going to the Bentons' house because it felt safe. It turns out that after the kids went to bed Tom and Betty got down to some serious weirdness with my parents involving various drugs, but their evening wildness did not threaten the reassuring structure that their children lived within, in contrast to the formlessness of my life at Owl Farm. Their kids had chores and they all ate dinner together at the same time every night at the dinner table. We never sat down as a family, and never at the same time. They had rules: they had to be home by dinnertime, they had to clean their rooms regularly, and they had to do their homework before friends came over. I had just a few rules: don't wake Hunter up, don't touch the guns, and put the tools away when I used them. My chores were random and on-demand. In a kitchen drawer the Bentons had Pinwheels, those chocolate-covered marshmallows, and we could each have one—but only one, and not right before dinner. I didn't have much junk food at home, but there were no rules governing it. At the Bentons' the guidelines were clear and reasonable, and when they were violated the consequences were consistent. At my house the guidelines were unclear, the enforcement patchy, and the consequences vague and frightening. I envied Brian and Michelle's structured life and felt calm and safe there.

The Bentons also had cable TV, and when I went to their house we would watch *I Dream of Jeannie* or other programs that were not available at home on the one channel out of Grand Junction that we received out at Owl Farm. Some weekend nights I would stay the night and Brian, Michelle, and I would watch terrible horror movies, like *The Blob*, or movies about giant ants, or crickets, or spiders attacking New York City. It was wonderful.

At some point I stopped spending solitary nights at the Hotel Jerome and would instead be dropped off at the Bentons' while Sandy and Hunter went on to the bar. We would play games like hide-and-seek in the gallery after it closed. At one point Brian and I became obsessed with trucker culture. We memorized the "10" codes (such as "10-4") used by police and truckers, persuaded our parents to buy us CB radios, ordered stacks of brochures from truck manufacturing companies, and spent hours and hours in the Bentons' VW bus pretending to be truckers. The more the situation at home deteriorated, the more the Bentons became a refuge of stability for me. It was easy for me to imagine them as the perfect '70s family: somewhat weird, essentially normal, and happy together.

That ideal burst with the Bentons' divorce about a year before my mother and I left Hunter. Overnight, it seemed, they sold the house in town, and Betty and the kids were suddenly in California while Tom stayed in Aspen with his girlfriend, the soon-to-be-ex-wife of a good friend of Hunter's and fellow resident of Woody Creek. My mother and I hadn't seen Betty and the kids since they left, thus our visit to California.

This trip was the beginning of an entirely new life and a new adventure for my mother and me. We were returning to the state where I was born and where my parents were happiest together, and where Hunter wrote his first book, which transformed him from a reporter to a writer.

I didn't think about this at the time. I was glad to be on an adventure and mostly I was glad that we were safe and away from my father. I didn't miss him at all.

We took several days to make the drive to California, staying at little motels. One day we stopped in Reno at Harrah's Automobile Collection to see the beautiful old classic cars, and bought a large black-and-white photo of a long, sleek black convertible that ended up on the wall at Owl Farm for years. I wonder now if my mother bought it as a gift for Hunter even while fleeing him. I remember driving through the heat and brown of the Nevada desert, and the next day through the Central Valley of California and being amazed at how green everything was. Mostly I remember the feeling of freedom and the sudden absence of fear and anxiety. My mother and I were away from that beast in Aspen. He couldn't touch us; he didn't even know where we were. We were safe and we were having an adventure. If my mother was concerned about money or jobs or a place to live, she didn't tell me.

We got to Betty's house, which was on the side of a steep hill overlooking San Anselmo. I remember how lush it was there. The house was white and surrounded by flowers, bushes, and trees of all kinds. Colorado had nothing like this. We spent two weeks in suburban peace. There was no screaming, no threats, no police, no hiding. Betty worked during the day and came home in the evening. The kids attended public school nearby and had neat rooms of their own with big windows that overlooked the valley below. Everything was clean, orderly, quiet, and beautiful in that early summer in Marin County.

At the end of two weeks I got on a plane in San Francisco and joined my grandmother in New York, and from there we went to Ireland for a couple of weeks. Ever since I was ten my grandmother Leah, who was a travel agent in DeLand, Florida, had taken me every summer on a trip to foreign lands. It was back when travel agents didn't have computers and the airlines gave them great discounts on flights. One year it was England, another year Paris, a third year Greece and Italy. That year it was Ireland and Scotland. We went to Dublin, Edinburgh, and Inverness, I kissed the Blarney Stone and took a boat ride on Loch Ness, and for two weeks I didn't think about my family.

I had a surprise awaiting me back in the United States. Sandy met me at the airport in New York and told me that we were going home to Owl Farm. Hunter had come for her, she said, and now things were going to be different. There would be no more fighting, no more police in the middle of the night. Hunter was going to change because he didn't want to lose us. I went along with it, full of apprehension. I was relieved that we would be back at home but fearful that nothing would change.

The three of us stayed on in New York for a few days more. I remember driving out to Long Island with Hunter and Sandy one afternoon to a house in the middle of a forest. I was introduced to a guy named John Belushi, and while he talked with my parents, I sat on the couch with another guy named Bill Murray. He seemed to prefer to talk to me rather than to the other adults, and he was interesting, odd, calm, quiet, and not condescending. I liked him. We talked about sailing.

We returned home to Owl Farm. I changed schools and started eighth grade at the Aspen Community School, now located about a quarter mile from home up on a mesa. Every morning, I would climb the steep hill to the top of the mesa and walk across the open fields to school.

That summer we attended Jimmy Buffett's—Captain Buffett's—wedding. He and Jane were getting married outside of Aspen at an old estate from the Colorado mining days called the Redstone Castle. While in New York Sandy had taken me to a tailor who measured me for a child-size white tuxedo with a royal blue cummerbund. I even had a walking stick. I'm sure I was the only child at that wedding reception, which I learned much later was an evening of high debauchery, '70s style, with copious amounts of cocaine, pot, and booze along with handfuls of pills, mushrooms, and tabs of acid. Oblivious to all of this, I strolled around the grounds of the estate like a diminutive English lord and threaded my way through the crowded and increasingly unstrung crowd in the ballroom. I explored every room (except the bedrooms—who knew who might be having a licit or illicit liaison in one of them), the hallways and staircases, examined all the outbuildings, and eventually curled up with a book until my parents found me and took me home.

For a while it was as if my mother and I had never left Hunter. We all took our places and resumed the routine, without the late-night fights. We didn't talk about what had happened, there were no family therapy sessions, we just picked up as if the police had never come and our trip to California had just been a summer vacation to visit some friends.

But of course it couldn't last. Nothing had changed underneath, so the old dynamics reasserted themselves and the fighting began again, along with the screaming, the crashing of glass or pottery, Hunter's verbal brutality, and Sandy's tearful hysteria. I stood again in the kitchen, an observer and harsh judge of my father when the fights were too loud and long to bear in the darkness of my bedroom. Otherwise, I huddled down in my bed and tried not to hear what I was hearing. It seemed as if we could do this forever.

But it became too much even for us, a family that had become accustomed to such unhappiness. One night my mother called the police again, and this time two troopers from the Colorado State Patrol came, a man and a woman. Hunter took the same approach he had before, calmly assuring them that my mother was drunk and raving, and that there was no need to get involved. I stood by in my pajamas, growing angrier and angrier. Sandy told Hunter that she and I were going to leave that night. She took a drawer of her clothes from her room and began to carry it to the front door. Hunter accused her of stealing from him and wrenched it from her. I started screaming at him, calling him a bastard, an asshole, and I lunged at him to beat on him with my undersized fists. One of the troopers grabbed me and held me until I stopped. At that moment I understood my mother's feeling of helplessness in the face of his strength, his intelligence, his lies, and his malice, and I hated him. I hated him deeply and completely. If I could have called down a god's wrath on him and destroyed him with a lightning bolt at that moment, I would have done it. He was more than frightening, he was deliberately and carefully cruel—he was evil—and I would have destroyed him if I could have, for my sake and for my mother's.

The police kept Hunter at bay while my mother and I grabbed a few clothes and got in the car. Now Hunter was powerless to stop us. The two most important people in his life were leaving him, and for once, he could not stop it from happening. Hunter was losing his cool. He didn't get violent, but he kept up a stream of insults and threats against both my mother and the police until we drove away. I don't know where we went that night. I don't know what we took with us, but it couldn't have been much.

A few days later I went back out to Owl Farm with a policeman to get some of my things. Even now, that police escort is surreal. A police escort to my own home? Did my mother request this? What did the police think was going to happen? That he would try to prevent me from taking my clothes as he had tried to stop my mother?

It got even stranger as we approached the driveway. I saw police cars parked along the road, and police scattered across the hillside, some with rifles, as if this was a hostage situation with a lunatic gunman. Did they think Hunter was going to break out the kitchen window, shove a high-powered rifle barrel through the opening, and start shooting wildly? Sure, my father was weird. Sure, he loved guns, and yes, he had a ferocious temper and a capacity for real cruelty. But a SWAT team on the hillside? Even in my rage at and fear of my father, I knew he would not hurt me. I didn't want to have to talk to him that day, I hated him, I was terrified of him, but I was never afraid he would hurt me. The much more likely problem was the presence of lots of armed policemen around his house. I can't imagine anything more provocative than surrounding his house with police sharpshooters, except maybe kicking in the front door and dragging him to jail. Fortunately, he wasn't at home. He must have been warned by friends of the situation and seen the wisdom of sidestepping the whole crazy scene. I quickly got my clothes, got back in the police car, and returned to my mother in town.

That was it, the final separation and the end of our life as a family, such as we were. Sandy and I moved into Aspen, eventually renting a house in the West End with a roommate while Hunter stayed at Owl Farm. Life was the same in many ways, and yet totally different. I still attended the Community School on the mesa overlooking my home, but now I took the bus from Aspen. I had the same friends, but now we played in Aspen instead of out in the country. In the afternoon I took the bus into Aspen. As we turned the corner onto the main road, I could see my old driveway out the window and watch it recede. There were still men in our new home in Aspen, but they were roommates or my mother's boyfriends, not my father. And they were nice men, calm and attentive, who didn't yell and break things in the middle of the night.

FIVE

THE IN-BETWEEN TIME: AGES 13 TO 18

The ugly divorce—Drugs and vandalism—Andover, Concord, the call
of the East—Movie night with Dad—Cleaning the guns—Hawaii

HST TIMELINE

1978   HST and Sandy Thompson separate, initiate divorce
        proceedings.

1979   *The Great Shark Hunt* (compilation) published. Hunter starts
        spending a lot of time in Key West.

1980   *Where the Buffalo Roam* movie released. Hunter and Ralph
        Steadman go to Hawaii to cover the Honolulu Marathon. This
        adventure becomes the book *The Curse of Lono.*

1981   HST starts working on a novel, *The Silk Road,* based on the
        Mariel Boatlift. This book is never completed.

1982   *The Curse of Lono* published.

PAUL RUBIN was my drama coach in eighth and ninth
grades at the Aspen Community School. He directed such
ambitious school plays as *One Flew Over the Cuckoo's Nest* and
Blues for Mister Charlie with a cast of completely inexperienced
eight-to-fourteen-year-olds. He told me that one day he and
Hunter were at the Jerome Bar, and Hunter told him that my
birthday was coming up and asked Paul if he had any idea what

I might like. Paul told him that during breaks from rehearsals for our current play a bunch of the kids played catch, and that perhaps a baseball glove might be a good thing, since I didn't have one. Hunter thanked him, walked down to Carl's Pharmacy, and bought a baseball glove for me. On my birthday he gave it to me. Hunter saw Paul afterward and told him that I looked at the glove, tried it on, took it off, and said, "I'm *left*-handed."

I don't remember this at all. Maybe it happened, maybe it didn't. Maybe it was some other kid. Other people's memories are no more reliable than mine. Hunter would no doubt remember it, because he remembered nearly everything, but I can't ask him now. Assuming it's true, though, it sums up where things stood. We had a long way to go.

Divorce proceedings began, which would drag on for the next five years. For the first couple of years Sandy would tell me about the rotten things Hunter and his lawyer were doing to her. I was a willing audience. None of his tactics or offenses surprised me, they only confirmed what I knew: that he was a bad, bad man. At one point there was talk of me testifying in divorce court, but thankfully that never came to pass. Thankfully also, there was never a custody battle. Hunter and Sandy had agreed from the start that I would live with my mother and see Hunter if and when I wished.

And for the next couple of years I did not wish to see him. At the same time my mother began dating and this brought new father figures into my life.

In one sense, my parents' divorce was the best thing that could have happened to my relationship with Hunter. For one thing, there were no more of those nightmarish fights. Sandy would gripe and bitch now and then about Hunter's lawyers and his resistance to meeting her demands, but this was mild. Yes, it helped to confirm that Hunter was a bastard, but in a distant and abstract way, as opposed to being in the room while they fought and watching my father use his whole array of psychological weapons to beat my mother down to a sobbing wreck.

His absence also revealed to me my need for a father.

I was grateful, on one hand, to get out of that house full of hatred, desperation, and misery, but it was also my home. In those last years at Owl Farm, I was happiest when I was away from it. Once I left for good, though, I was drawn back to it. It was the place where I grew up. I knew the house and the land intimately. It was always my real home, whether I was living in Aspen, Carbondale, Boston, England, or Boulder. It was home in a different sense of the word, in the sense of my roots, rather than my dwelling. I didn't want to live there with Hunter, but I always wanted to be able to return. I still do.

What had changed was that he and I could no longer take each other's presence for granted in the hope that somehow a real and living relationship of mutual love and respect would magically spring up between us as long as we lived in the same house. Once we were separated, I longed to be with him, though once there, neither he nor I knew what to do.

When I did see him, I remember how strange it was to be back in the house as a guest, and yet it was still my home. For a while my room remained unchanged. It was like being a ghost, returning after a sudden death to haunt the places that I had lived, seeking, in accordance with some deep natural law beyond appeal, some kind of resolution or undoing of the past. As the house changed gradually (my room was turned into a guest room, a piece of furniture changed now and then, sometimes a whole room changed), I would still seek out those places and things that tied me to the time when I had lived there. For years and years

I would at some point during my visit go into the basement, into the big, dark storage room beneath the kitchen, and browse among memories. I wasn't looking for anything in particular, I was reminiscing, revisiting toys, books, tools, musical instruments, anything that had been part of our home up until our separation and that could link me back to that time.

When I went to visit, Hunter would make an effort to be available. And I was no longer trying to reduce my visibility as an accidental or convenient target. I was there to see my father. Therefore we had to have something to do. One activity we did together was clean guns. He had many guns and he shot most of them frequently. Cleaning them was laborious but necessary. It became a bonding ritual between us that lasted up until the day of his death.

It began one movie night, another ritual that gave us a reason to be together. It was the three of us, Hunter, myself, and Laila Nabulsi, his lovely, young live-in girlfriend and later fiancée. They never married, but she lived at Owl Farm for several years and played an important part in both stabilizing Hunter after the divorce and helping Hunter and me begin to move toward each other.

Hunter would set up the TV in the living room on a rolling cart, select a classic movie, often a Bogart film, turn the lights off, and we would enjoy some quality family time. Before one of these nights Hunter brought out a couple of guns and said that they needed to be cleaned. He gathered up the cleaning supplies—solvent, cleaning pads, brushes, rods, and gun oil— and proceeded to teach me. We started with a pistol that Hunter disassembled and then passed the pieces to me to clean. He would clean one gun while I worked on another. He patiently explained the proper way to clean the parts, and how to disassemble and reassemble the guns. I was anxious to learn, anxious to please, and honored to be taking part in the ritual of gun cleaning, which was unmistakably a kind of rite of passage. Looking back on it, there was a lot in common between learning to clean the guns and learning to turn a winch, reef a sail, or scrub the icebox on the boat with Jimmy Buffett. Except in this case, it was my real father teaching me, not a stand-in. I was determined to do it just right and cleaned each piece as thoroughly as I possibly could. After I finished with each piece, Hunter would examine it and pronounce it good, or point out an area I had missed. I was happy for any kind of patient attention from Hunter, even if it involved pointing out my mistakes. By the end of the movie that night we would have had a couple of guns clean and oiled, and Hunter would put them away.

Many years later when Jennifer, Will, and I would go to visit him at Owl Farm, he would tell me within minutes that there were guns to clean since my last visit. I did not ask if I could clean them, he did not ask me to clean them. At some point in the evening I might say something like, "Time to clean some guns," and Hunter would say, "Good! Clean that nickel-plated twelve-gauge, it's filthy." I would ask if there were any others to be added to the list. As he got older I think he stopped cleaning the guns, yet he still felt a gun owner's guilt for not taking care of them properly. I know he was delighted when I would clean them, both because I clearly appreciated them, and because he could let himself off the hook for at least that one small thing.

Sometimes we would shoot. I remember shooting clay pigeons together. I remember cartons of yellow or orange clay pigeons on the porch, and Hunter and his friends shooting while someone flung them with a handheld launcher. Later the yard and the field beyond it were littered with fragments of clay pigeons.

Shooting was something that bound us. I don't know what kind of boy Hunter had expected, but I'm pretty sure I wasn't what he had in mind. He was fascinated by sports and had been since he was a boy. I had no interest in sports. He was very social, drank too much, raised hell, and got laid. I was quiet and shy, got drunk a few times a year with some friends, and was most definitely a virgin.

The guns connected us. I love the power of guns and the elegance and precision of the engineering, especially in the revolvers and side-by-side shotguns. The machining is so fine, the fit of the parts so precise, the movement of the parts so smooth. The gun itself can be a work of art, whatever you might think about its purpose, usefulness, or danger. For an admirer of the mechanical craft, a well-made gun is a thing of beauty. Hunter shared this appreciation for the machine itself. As I got older I came to appreciate the power, particularly of large handguns such as the Ruger .44 Magnum and the Freedom Arms .454 Casull.

What do fathers want most from their sons? Do we only want them to be happy? Do we want them to be like us? Do we want forgiveness? Do we want them to be better than us in love, work, money, fatherhood? Do we want to be loved by our sons? Is it enough that they want to still talk to us when they grow up? I don't know what my father wanted from me. He was happy when I graduated with honors from college; he was happy when I got married to a woman he respected; he was thrilled when my son came along. I know he was glad I was able to support myself and that I wasn't a drunk or a drug addict. I know he needed my forgiveness.

I don't know what he wanted. And yet, it's so terribly important to me to believe that I didn't let him down. He's dead, I'm in middle age, and it's still very important. Will there be a time when I can say it doesn't matter what my father thought of me? I don't think so, not today. I see it in my own son. He doesn't want to disappoint me, wants me to be proud of him, so much so that he won't tell me things that he thinks might upset me. I tell him that he can tell me anything and I'm not going to get angry at him, but he doesn't always believe me. I ask myself if I have done anything to make him fear me or think I would disapprove. Maybe it's just the nature of fathers and sons.

As Hunter and I began the long, long road to reconciliation, the separation and move into Aspen brought new father figures into my life. Sandy dated a nice man, Bill, who owned an art gallery in Aspen. He would come for dinner and stay the night. We spent a Christmas together. He paid attention to me. He was calm and thoughtful. When they stopped dating I was sorry to see him go.

After Bill there was Don, with whom we ended up living for the next few years. Don was more like an older brother than a father. He was probably around thirty and Sandy was forty. He was funny, lighthearted, earnest, and he knew how to have fun. We took to each other right away. When I talked to him for this book, he said that he came over for dinner one night while Bill was out of town, and never left. The next morning Sandy went to work and Don and I sat at the dining room table playing a game with a little folded-up triangle of paper in which we would try to flick the triangle through the goalposts of the other person's fingers. We didn't talk much, just played this game for an hour or so. It must have been a very uncomfortable situation. As far as I knew, Bill was the boyfriend, and suddenly here's this new guy who spent the night and he and I are alone while Sandy goes off to work. Sandy did not explain why he was there, or what was going to happen when Bill returned, or how Don fit into our lives.

Fortunately we got along well. Sandy broke up with Bill and Don essentially moved in, though he kept his apartment for a while. We went camping in his old Toyota Land Cruiser, went sledding in the winter, had picnics in the summer. On weekend mornings we went out to breakfast and read the papers. One day after a particularly large snowstorm we jumped out the second-story window into the deep snow in the backyard, over and over again, laughing and laughing.

Hunter didn't talk to me about Sandy or Don when I went to visit him, but apparently he knew about him. Don told me a story about the first time that he met Hunter, when he discovered that she was still married, and to, of all people, the infamous Hunter Thompson. Early in their relationship, he and Sandy were awakened late one night by an insistent pounding on the door. Sandy went to the door and found Hunter there, very angry, with a shotgun in his hand. She and Hunter argued for a while until Don couldn't stand it any longer and went to try to help her. He saw Hunter with the shotgun, walked up to him, put two fingers in the barrel, and slowly took it away from him. The crisis was defused, and after a bit more talk, Hunter left and Sandy and Don returned to bed. I think there were very few people who had the courage to take a gun away from an angry Hunter S. Thompson. I also am sure that the gun was not loaded.

Though I didn't see Hunter much during those years, Don did tell me about a time when I met him and Sandy in Honduras after staying with Hunter for a week or so in the Florida Keys. He said that I arrived traumatized and withdrawn from that visit, and that it took several days for me to unwind. Taking LSD with

With Sandy and Don Stuber in 1978. Don was
like my fun, kind, gentle older brother.

Don and floating in the bay at night off the shore of a Honduran island may have helped that process.

It was with Don that I first took LSD, aka acid, when I was around fourteen. Like many people in the '70s, he was interested in Eastern spirituality, and this shaped his approach to taking acid. Like Hunter, Don approached acid as a ceremonial drug, not a party drug. My first time was with Sandy, Don, my best friend Brad Laboe, and me. We had a ceremony before taking the acid. I remember putting the acid blotters on a pillow and sitting on the floor. There may have been candles. There was certainly a sense of respect and solemnity as we embarked on this new journey. Don, Brad, and I took the acid and Sandy remained straight. She was to be the trip master, the one adult who was straight, who could take care of things when needed, not to mention drive. We went to the Glenwood Springs hot springs pool that night. It may have been wintertime, so the steam would have been thick over the pool and there were few people there. As trip master, Sandy took care of mundane things like paying admission, keeping track of the car, handling the ordering of food when we went to a restaurant after swimming. It was a wonderful, magical experience. We laughed and laughed, had insights, discovered new things or saw them in new ways. Another time Sandy, Don, Brad, and I went to the Telluride Bluegrass Festival. We all took acid and while Sandy and Don lay on the ground and listened to the music, Brad and I went wandering around the festival grounds and the town with a notebook, the "Acid Notebook." I remember at the time we were overflowing with insights. I also remember that when we looked at the notebook the next day, it made no sense whatsoever.

When I told my wife, Jennifer, about these experiences years later, she was appalled, both by the fact that at fourteen I was taking acid, and worse, that my mother was actively supporting it. I also remember hearing that someone once asked Hunter at a lecture how he would react if he found out his son had taken acid. He responded, "I'd beat the shit out of him." I did not talk to Hunter about my drug use then or in fact ever. And he never asked. He didn't want to know.

Don and I were good friends. He was the opposite of Hunter in almost every way I can think of. He was safe, he listened, I never saw him lose his temper. He laughed a lot. We did things together all the time. He did not have separate worlds that he would move back and forth between with little or no communication between them. He didn't forget birthdays; he drank occasionally but not heavily or regularly. He was kind. He didn't care for sports. He was up on the latest music and introduced us to a new realm, called "new wave," whereas Hunter, though also a music lover, was rooted in the music of the '60s and '70s with an emphasis on rock, southern rock, jazz, and folk, people like Joan Baez, The Rolling Stones, Herbie Mann, Bob Dylan, and The Allman Brothers Band. Don liked to dance, and he and Sandy would often go to the local disco. Though he aspired to be a professional photographer, his day job was fine woodwork in Aspen. He didn't travel for his job, he went to work in the morning and returned in the evening. He went to sleep before midnight and was up by seven a.m. A couple of years later I worked for him one summer as an apprentice and he taught me the rudiments of fine carpentry. He had a job I could see, the results were tangible, and it didn't consume his life. I don't know if he and Sandy discussed it, but it seems now that he had decided he would not try to take on the role of a father, but be a friend instead. And he did that extremely well. He gave me attention, love, friendship, stability, and safety at a time when I desperately needed it. Hunter was my father, physically, spiritually, and mythologically, but we were not friends. Don was not my father, but he was my friend.

During those teenage years when I was living in Aspen I started doing stupid things. My friends and I got the idea to go out on a weekend night and cause trouble. We began by drinking. If we were at a friend's house we would sneak the booze from the liquor cabinet, but if we were at my house there was no need to be secretive. We would announce that we were going out, and then pour a drink, sometimes with Sandy and Don joining us.

Then my friends and I went out. At first, walking through the alleys on our way downtown, we were intrigued by the main electrical cutoff switches on the apartment buildings. We discussed them, then examined them and found that very few were locked. We made our getaway plans, then one of us grabbed the switch and pulled it down. There was a clunk as the switch disengaged, and then all the lights in the building went off. We ran like hell, cranked up on adrenaline and fear. Several blocks away, gasping for air, we reveled in our cleverness. We kept this up for a few months, just a few buildings at a time, and not every weekend, maybe once a month. One night, we walked through the alley behind a very popular disco, the Paragon. We had become attuned to the presence of main cutoff switches and noticed the Paragon's. There was no lock. We planned the route. The music was loud, the simple thump of the disco beat was like a heartbeat. One of us grabbed the big handle and pulled down. The music suddenly stopped. There was a second of silence, and then the sound of a hundred voices all crying out in fear and confusion at once. We split and scattered, meeting up again several blocks away. No one followed us. We were very proud of ourselves. Over the next week we heard from others how the Paragon had gone dark Saturday night, and we were even more pleased. Several weeks later we decided it would be safe to do it again. We did not realize that we had inspired a rash of copycat shutoffs, and that the Paragon management was now prepared.

Again we laid out our plan and pulled the switch. This time, within a couple of seconds, two bouncers burst out the back door and took off after us. Our escape route was not well planned. We ran into a drugstore nearby and stood, panting, in the aisle. A bouncer followed us in, grabbed us, and marched us over to the police station. As we walked, he lectured us on the dangers of what we had done: Did we realize we were putting lives at risk? What if there had been a surgery in progress somewhere in the building? Had we thought of that? This struck me as a bad example, but it was not the time to point this out. The officer on duty threatened to call our parents. He must have seen the look of fear on our faces, because he relented, and said that because we were first offenders he would let us off, but that he better never see us again in that office. It worked. We stayed far away from the Paragon and cutoff switches in general.

Instead, we moved to petty vandalism. One night we started bending car antennas. We were a bit drunk and maybe stoned, and it was funny. We either broke them off if they were the hollow extending type, or bent them into shapes if they were the solid, flexible type. It was late and there was no one on the street in these neighborhoods, so we hit a lot of cars that night. Over that summer we did this several times and once it even appeared in the police blotter of the local newspaper. We graduated to bending windshield wipers back on themselves, so that they were facing the sky rather than the window. Every now and then we would turn off the power to a house, or move a small car into the middle of a quiet street. We thought those were funny pranks too, and we were never caught.

That was our last summer of vandalism. Maybe it was the ugly pointlessness of it, maybe the promptings of our consciences became sufficiently strong, or maybe I got over my need to rebel against being a good boy. Whatever the reason, thankfully we stopped.

Hunter never did find out. For all his wildness and crazy pranks, I know that if he had found out I was up to such petty, stupid mischief he would have been furious (though the Paragon he might have appreciated—once), and worse, he would have been disappointed. He appreciated smart jokes with a purpose, but not dumb vandalism. That was for half-bright punks with no imagination and nothing worthwhile to say. As he wrote to a young fan, Dale, after the publication of *Hell's Angels,* who wrote to tell him he wanted to be a Hells Angel: "They're not smart, or funny, or brave, or even original. They're just Old Punks. . . .

[who are] not bright enough to create their own scene. . . ." His parting advice to Dale was "Be an outlaw . . . but do it your own way, for your own reasons . . ." He might have added, "and for the right reasons." There was nothing smart, funny, brave, or original about wandering around Aspen half drunk bending antennas and wipers, though it seemed that way at the time. I'm still ashamed of it.

I was also preparing for high school. I never seriously considered staying in Aspen. I wanted to go to boarding school, an East Coast boarding school. I had grand ideas as a boy about the life I wanted to lead, or more accurately the way I wanted it to look, and I knew for sure that Aspen High School was not part of that picture. That was the jungle where kids lived by the Law of Claw and Fang, and where smart, short, shy kids with bowl haircuts— full-fledged nerds such as myself—got teased, picked on, and occasionally beat up. I wanted to be part of a higher, finer world with large, old houses filled with fine, expensive, delicate things, with vast, perfectly trimmed green lawns sloping down to a lake or an ocean or a thick green forest. Aspen in the '70s was a rural, small western ski town with a pinch of academia courtesy of The Aspen Institute, and a hefty dose of Haight-Ashbury's rejection of all norms and rules. I wanted something completely different. I wanted to be elegant, rich, aristocratic, and traditional.

This is just what Hunter had grown up with and then fled from in Louisville. His friends at the Athenaeum Literary Association embodied these qualities as scions of wealthy old Louisville families, bound for Ivy League colleges and then to careers in law, business, or government, absolutely soaked in traditions, elegance, and wealth. Hunter had a paradoxical relationship with tradition. On one hand he was a breaker of icons, traditions, and beliefs. On the other hand he was a southern gentleman who grew up in a comfortable middle-class Kentucky home where he learned the essential rules of polite southern society. Hunter had disdain for a life lived according to social expectations, yet he was angry when, upon meeting some friends of his, I did not shake hands and take part in the ritual of greeting. He did not realize that I was completely ignorant of these rituals, being brought up with no training in manners whatsoever.

Though Hunter approved of a certain amount of tradition, he certainly didn't endorse elite education. He had barely graduated from Louisville Male High School because of his lack of interest and never had much good to say about formal schooling. My mother had gone to a Quaker boarding school on Long Island but she rarely mentioned it since it referred to the privileged Long Island upbringing that she had repudiated. Her father and brother had both gone to Choate Rosemary Hall but at that time she had nothing but contempt for both of them, establishment bourgeoisie that they were. I had decided to apply to some of the best, most exclusive boarding schools: Andover, Groton, and Concord Academy. Sandy and I went east that summer of 1978 to look at schools. We looked at a bunch, Andover and Concord being my favorites. I did my interviews, sent in my applications, and waited until spring.

I ended up getting accepted to both Andover and Concord Academy. I picked Concord. I told Sandy, but I never told Hunter directly. I never asked for his advice. But then I had never asked for his advice in the past. We were not friends, and he had neither the familiarity with my life nor the authority to give me advice. Looking at it now, it is a shame that we knew each other so little at that point. I wish it had been otherwise. I wish I had asked his advice. I think now he would have said going East was a terrible idea, that I didn't belong there, and that where I went to school didn't say a damn thing about me. But I had to find out for myself.

I went to Concord Academy, and it was hell. I was short, about five feet, with a bowl haircut, and wearing things like plaid shirts with turtlenecks, corduroys, and canvas sneakers. I showed up the first day at Concord wearing jeans and a down vest. My roommates wore oxford button-downs and penny loafers. I had no training in manners or socializing. I was truly a stranger in a strange land. I had just come from a tiny private school where my graduating ninth-grade class consisted of eight other students with whom I shared all classes and activities. That school was essentially a giant log cabin in the middle of hay fields on the mesa next to Owl Farm. We went on several backpacking trips each year, some for up to ten days through the mountains of Colorado. The last year Brad and I had studied bomb-making with George Stranahan, the physicist and benefactor of the school, and had successfully set off a large pipe bomb packed with gunpowder in a gopher hole outside the school. On our last camping trip before graduation, all the eighth and ninth graders sat in a circle and each person told every other person in the circle what they appreciated about them, something that took several hours and was very emotional. Though I was shy by nature, I knew these people so well, and the school was so small, that there was no room for shyness. Since we had the same two teachers for every class and almost every activity, the students were very close to the teachers. We were like a family. My ninth-grade diploma was mimeographed, and the school director gave us each a small sapling as a graduation gift.

From here I went to Concord, Massachusetts, a small and wealthy New England town just outside of Boston. Concord and nearby Lexington were the sites of the first battles in the Revolutionary War, the site of Walden Pond, and the residence of Thoreau, Emerson, Hawthorne, and Louisa May Alcott, among others. The town is still over 90 percent white with a median family income of $115,000. In addition to Concord Academy, there was one other prep school as well as two private schools for the lower grades, one of which was all-boys and the other all-girls after third grade. The countryside itself was foreign. It was flat, and lush with trees, bushes, and flowers. I had never seen so many huge leafy trees. There was no mountain horizon, just trees. The houses were old and delicate colonial homes of clapboard or brick, not the ranch or farmhouses I was used to. Concord was a perfect example of the traditional New England elitism that I was seeking—and that I had absolutely nothing in common with.

Hunter apparently understood that this transition was going to be difficult for me. He contacted his good friends, Richard and Doris Kearns Goodwin, who lived in Concord a few miles from the school. Hunter arranged for me to be able to visit them on weekends if I needed friends or a place to go. I am sure now that he also wanted someone to keep an eye on me and let him know how I was doing. He did the same thing three years later when I returned to Boston to attend Tufts University.

Sandy flew to Concord with me and helped me get established. In the dorm I shared a large room with two roommates. Sandy bought furnishings so that my corner of the room was marked off by a carpet and a bookshelf. I had brought my computer, a Radio Shack TRS-80, and set it up on the bookshelf. I had no idea how to deal with these two foreigners in my room. I tried to ignore them, and they left me alone, though at least once one of them invited me to join him and some of his friends for ice cream. I declined. One day I came into the room and saw a few people standing around my computer and using it. I angrily chased them off. I spent my days in isolation. One day there was a trip to the beach for all the new students. I went, because I had to, and I found a large rock some distance from the rest of the kids and read my book (I was working through Tolkien's *Lord of the Rings* trilogy) for the entire afternoon. I'm sure I read on the bus ride both ways so I could avoid talking to anyone. At meals I read my book in solitude. After classes I read my book before and after doing my homework. I had no social skills and no confidence. I was utterly, pathetically lonely and homesick. I would call my mother daily and plead with her to let me come home. She finally told me that I would have to talk to Hunter.

I remember calling him one afternoon from a phone booth in downtown Concord, down the street from the school. I told him how miserable I was and how I wanted to come back to Aspen. He tried to convince me to stick it out. He said this was the predictable homesickness that most kids feel when they go away for the first time, and he said it would pass. I begged him, I sobbed, I pleaded, I told him I couldn't do it. We talked for a long time. Finally he agreed to let me come home.

This is one of those questions I wish I could ask him now. Why did you agree to let me come home? Did you understand how completely unprepared I was to be away from home? What do you think would have happened if you had insisted that I stay for the entire year? Who did you think I was then?

I was fifteen, it was 1979, and Hunter was with Laila. As part of my research for this book, I asked Laila what she remembered. She said that Hunter wanted me to have a good education, and that he was upset at the prospect of losing at least $5,000 in tuition, but that he understood how difficult it must have been for me, an only and very sensitive child, to be so far away from home only a year or so after the collapse of our family, and in the midst of an acrimonious divorce. It may be that he understood me better than I did, that he knew or suspected that it was too much for me to handle two such major ordeals in such a short time.

I had never considered that possibility until Laila told me. How ironic that he, who hardly spoke to me, whom I saw so rarely, who had played virtually no part in the major decisions affecting my life, should comprehend my predicament better than I did, and that only now, decades later, after his death, I should come to have compassion for that boy who was going through very difficult times.

There is no knowing what would have happened had I stayed, but odds are I would have remained utterly miserable until the end of that school year and then refused to return the following year. Furthermore, I was melded with my mother. I could not imagine daily life without her. In contrast, I have watched my son gradually distance himself, one tiny step at a time, from his mother. When he was six he was able to tolerate separations that at four would not have been possible. As he has become a teenager, he is more likely to disagree with her, to risk her anger. He is not gregarious, but he reaches out into the world with more and more confidence and can stand alone. I did not have that confidence. I was my mother's confidant, her trusted, devoted, attentive, and sympathetic friend who needed her desperately. In turn, she was my biggest fan and cheerleader, the one person who loved me completely. How could I live without her?

After getting Hunter's assent, I started marking off the days. In order to get a tuition refund, I had to stay until a certain date. On that day, Hunter came to pick me up. I remember that it was mid-morning and there was nobody in the dorm. I quickly packed up my things and loaded them into the rental car, hoping that no one would see me. I didn't tell my roommates; one morning I just disappeared. I never regretted leaving, though I tried the eastern experiment again for college three years later with marginally better success.

After Concord, I ended up as a day student at a private prep school in Carbondale, Colorado, called Colorado Rocky Mountain School, or CRMS, about thirty miles down-valley from Aspen. Sandy, Don, and I moved into a brand-new subdivision about a mile from school. It was a small ranch house in the classic suburban mold. Each day I would walk across pastures and climb the fences between the subdivision and school while Sandy and Don commuted to Aspen.

My experience at Concord was the result of a brutal collision between my fantasies of East Coast elitism and the reality of who I was and where I came from. CRMS was a much more suitable fit for many reasons. It was thirty miles from Aspen, which made my transition easier. I was a day student, so I had the pleasure of living with Sandy and Don another year. Finally, it was a different kind of school. It had been founded in the '60s as "an antidote to modern easy living." A ranch had been converted into a school, which the students had had a large part in building. Twice a week for two hours after classes all students were assigned to small groups that took care of some aspect of school maintenance, from cooking to washing dishes to fixing machinery to caulking the cracks in the old wooden buildings. The other three days we had a sport of some kind, from horseback riding to cross-country skiing to kayaking and soccer. In addition, every student was responsible for an assigned job. My best friend at CRMS, Stevens, was once on hog-feeding duty at six every morning in the winter. I once had bathroom-cleaning duty for a semester. These weren't punishments, they were jobs that needed to be done and the founders of the school felt that it was important for character development that the students do them. Finally, like my previous school, we did lots of backpacking in Colorado and Utah. Though I was still shy, I was able to make a friend in the first couple of weeks, and by the end of the year I was a part of the school community.

That year with Don and Sandy was, in a word, comfort. We went to breakfast every Saturday at the Village Smithy, a popular local restaurant in Carbondale. There were no arguments, no fights, no yelling. We went camping in Utah and took acid together several more times. The living room of our subdivision house was carpeted, with large bright windows. I loved to sit on the new carpet in the sun and read.

By the end of that year, though, the lease was up and my mother and Don were tired of living in a subdivision and commuting thirty miles each way to Aspen. We moved back to Aspen that summer and in the fall of 1980 I returned to CRMS, this time as a boarding student. I was apprehensive about boarding, but now it didn't seem quite so scary. I heard much later from Sandy that Hunter said at the time that I became a boarding student, "Best thing that could have happened to him." I didn't understand at the time how true that was. It wasn't until I was an adult that I saw that it was my first major step of independence from my mother and a step toward my father.

Hunter was paying far more attention to me than I thought. But if he was paying attention, why didn't he intervene occasionally? Maybe he did. Maybe he talked to my mother and told her to do this, to stop doing that. Maybe she listened, and maybe she did not. And maybe he did not intervene because he didn't trust himself, or because he was preoccupied with his own life. He was a self-centered man.

It was around this time that Deborah Fuller, who was to play such an important role in Hunter's life and in mine, entered the scene. Sandy and I had stayed with Deb and her teenage daughter, Kristine, for a summer in Aspen, in a large house she took care of. Through Sandy she met Hunter and began running errands for him for some extra cash. She was a very organized, very competent woman, a few years younger than Hunter, and within a year she was working for Hunter full-time, paying bills, buying groceries, organizing travel, and generally managing the day-to-day aspects of Hunter's life. She began doing the work for money, but over time she became a part of Hunter's life, and she took care of Hunter not because he paid her, but because she loved him, and he loved her. It was as if they were married, except it was not a romantic or a sexual relationship, it was a deep friendship that endured through many, many women and many hard times. I remember thinking often that it was as if Hunter was a polygamist, and Deb was the First Wife who had relinquished the conjugal duties to the younger women, yet had the longest history and the deepest bond with Hunter. The young women came and went, and Deb was always there, keeping Hunter's life on track, friendly with the women but loyal finally to Hunter. They were not lovers, they were not husband and wife, they were partners for twenty-four years. No one knew Hunter better in the daily manifestations of his complexity, and loved him more in spite of himself, than Deb. Hunter would not have made it to sixty-seven without her, and he and I would not have had the time we needed to find each other. Deb made that possible.

That winter Hunter proposed an assignment to *Running* magazine to cover the Honolulu Marathon. He and Ralph Steadman, along with Laila and Ralph's wife, Anna, rented a couple of houses in Kona, on the Big Island of Hawaii, and Hunter invited me to join them for Christmas.

I flew to L.A., stayed the night in the Hollywood Hills with Hunter's director friend Bob Rafelson, and flew to Hawaii the next day. The houses were right on the beach, or more accurately, the lava rock. Hawaii has two active volcanoes that periodically erupt and create huge tongues of slow-moving lava that creep down the sides of the mountains to the ocean, and then harden. This had apparently happened at one time where the houses were, because where the ocean met the land there was nothing but spiny black rock that only a fool would venture onto without thick shoes. A fall would result in serious lacerations. God help anyone who fell in the water and was caught between the surf and the lava. As Hunter documented in his book based on his time in Hawaii, *The Curse of Lono,* the weather was lousy. Large waves pounded the rock day and night.

I stayed for about two weeks. Ralph and Anna had already gone home, so it was just the three of us: Hunter, Laila, and me. It was uncharacteristically peaceful. I don't remember any crises, but a few memories stand out.

Fireworks were plentiful in Kona and Hunter had several "bombs," which consisted of five thousand firecrackers woven together into a belt that was rolled up into a disk more than a foot across and wrapped in bright red paper. During my stay I detached many from the end of one belt and set them off one by one, as I used to do when I was a boy at Owl Farm, blowing up plastic model cars, trucks, dirt hills, cans, anything that could be effectively ruptured. One night Hunter, Laila, myself, and several other people were having dinner at a seaside restaurant in Kona. I had a firecracker in my pocket, and I was feeling clever. While the rest of the people were talking, I took it from my pocket and pulled the fuse out of the body of the firecracker and attached it to the outside. I lit the fuse, and said, "Hey, Hunter! Here!" and threw the firecracker to him so that it landed in his lap, the little fuse sparkling. He cursed and frantically tried to brush it away before it exploded. But because the fuse was taped to the outside, it didn't explode, the fuse just burned to the end and stopped.

He had fallen for it, in front of other people, and he wasn't happy about it. He didn't yell or curse, but he didn't laugh either. He may have said, "You little bastard!" or flashed me that sudden artificial smile that was playful and yet slightly menacing. I remember thinking at the time that he was much better at being the originator of practical jokes than the recipient of them. It may have been a matter of pride. It was rare for him to be taken in; he was almost always the smartest guy in the room. I think he was also a little proud, though, that his son had been the one to do it.

My best memory from that trip is of golfing. One morning Hunter said, "Let's go golfing." I knew nothing about golf, Hunter knew that, but it was a chance for my father and me to spend some time together.

That morning we drove up the coast to a golf course. I don't remember seeing anyone else the entire time we were there. Hunter was pretty good, it seemed to me. He had played a fair amount as a kid in Louisville. I was hopeless, but that didn't matter. We were walking along lush green fairways that bordered cliffs that dropped down several hundred feet into the ocean. The morning was warm but not hot, the sky was clear and the air was hazy with humidity, soothing, and dreamlike. Hunter would give me pointers now and then on how to play. Though I'm sure he would have been happy had I been able to swing a club, he didn't seem to care. He was playing against himself, I was goofing. We played nine holes in three or four hours and then returned to the shack in Kona.

We hadn't had any profound talks in Hawaii, just quiet and unhurried time together, probably for the first time in many years, going back to before the bad years leading up to my parents' divorce. I'm sure there were questions he wanted to ask, and I could have asked him questions too, but I was just happy to be with my father when he was calm and patient, and I am sure that he didn't want to risk breaking the delicate filaments of connection that we were creating together on that trip, only somewhat consciously, with questions that could easily lead to anger, tears, and further distance. It was sacred time.

I was now at boarding school full-time and Sandy had embarked on a round-the-world tour that ended up lasting several years, with only occasional returns to the States. Hunter was paying my tuition on time for the most part. However, one day, several months into the school year, I was called to the headmaster's office and told that my father had not yet paid my tuition, and that if he did not do so immediately I would be kicked out. I felt a chill as I took it in. This had become my home. The notion of living with Hunter never even occurred to me—that would have been utter madness. In the past few years I had come to know and love the calm, the predictability, the stability of life without the grand drama of verbal death matches, imminent financial ruin, wild mood swings, and the ever-present fear of sudden outbursts of rage at any time.

I was very afraid of losing my new life, and I was also not surprised. By the time I was ten or so I had understood that Hunter

was irresponsible when it came to money. When I was still at
Owl Farm there was always the background threat of creditors
and not enough money. It seemed that he always owed the IRS
back taxes. Every so often it would come to a head, there would
be a scramble to come up with the money before something terrible happened, and then the threat would go away for a few
years. Credit cards were always coming and going—charged up,
ignored, canceled, paid off, and then reissued. I don't know how
many times American Express canceled and then later reissued a
card to Hunter, but it seems like dozens.

I was furious that his irresponsibility was threatening the stability of my life, not just his. I called him immediately and con-
veyed the threat from my headmaster. He promised to pay.

And he did. I did not hear from the headmaster again. In fact,
what strikes me now is that this happened so infrequently. I'm
sure he was late with tuition payments often, but that was the
only time it escalated to the point that I became aware of it. I
realize now that those sizable tuition payments were a high prior-
ity to him, right up there with the mortgage, the IRS, his cocaine
bill, and the Grog Shop liquor tab. As I read his letters from that
time, I realize that he was in a serious money crunch, between
his debts, a pending divorce settlement, and little income. His
correspondence with others around this time consists mostly of
schemes to make money quickly, either by selling book ideas or
selling part of Owl Farm. I now appreciate how serious he was
about my education.

My perception of my father was characterized by duality. It
was as if I saw my father through glasses whose lenses were two
different colors. There was the rose lens, the hero lens, and there
was the dark gray lens. Through the rose lens I saw Hunter as the
young, brilliant, brave, romantic, adventurous hero, and for all

my talk of wanting to be different, I wished I could be like him, my hero father. I read *Hell's Angels* in high school and I thought his description, at the end of the book, of driving the motorcycle down Highway 101 in the middle of the night was not only brilliantly written, but romantic, secret, and wonderful. I wanted that kind of life, and not only was Hunter writing about it, he was my father. Surely I had that potential in me, didn't I?

However, through the other lens I saw the raging monster, the man I could not count on, the man who burst into unpredictable fits of rage or who would yell suddenly for no good reason at all. This was the father who never paid his bills, who was never home, who cheated on my mother, and lied to the police.

I knew that he was both men, but I could only focus on one at a time. When people would ask me about him, I saw in my mind my hero father, a handsome young man who went seeking adventure on his motorcycle in the cool San Francisco nights, romancing beautiful women, having thoughtful and profound conversations with his friends while smoking a cigarette and looking out over the ocean, and then returning to his apartment to write, pipe clenched in his teeth, until the morning sun shone in through the window.

In private, though, when he let me down, I was ashamed of him, and I was filled with bitterness.

This duality persisted. Combining the two fantasies into one person was too complicated, too ambiguous, too paradoxical. I wanted a father I could love and adore, or a father I could put away from me for good.

But that's not how it works. There was one time in my freshman year at Tufts University in Boston when I was on the phone with Hunter at three a.m. or so. He was suggesting that he might not be able to pay for Tufts next year. However, the way he put it was something like, "You understand that if I have to choose between cigarettes and whiskey or your tuition, I'm going to buy cigarettes and whiskey." I held that comment against him for a long time. Why would he say such a thing? Perhaps it was a confession, that if it came down to a choice between his primary addictions and my tuition, he would have to choose the booze, not because he wanted to, but because he had to.

The fact is, though, that he did pay my tuition. When I later read letters from his archive, I saw that I was ignoring the circumstantial evidence, the important evidence. In a letter to Sandy in 1982 (when I was at Tufts) discussing the divorce settlement negotiations, he wrote, ". . . I intend to ignore [my divorce lawyer] for as long as possible (i.e. until I'm <u>forced</u> to seek legal counsel again). He's still bitching and Raving about the outrage of sending Juan to a school that costs a lot per year."

In another letter to his accountant, he notes that he has not received any parental mail from Tufts, and worries that the university administrators might look on me as a bad credit risk. He emphasizes how important it is that I not be worried by late tuition payments:

> That's what I want to avoid right now. Juan is going to get enough extra visibility just because he's my son—and it would be cruel (and maybe even too much pressure for him to handle) if he has to constantly live in fear about whether or not his tuition is paid up.
>
> So let's try to spare him these worries—for as long as we possibly can.
>
> Let's discuss this on the phone—but, ASAP, because I think it's very important for Juan's sake, to reassure the Tufts administration people that Juan is not a potential bad credit

problem and that we have taken all the normal and necessary
steps to pay his bill on schedule. . . . This initial $5K should
get us over the hump—(I think—although I'm not really sure
what it's for)—and I think we should use the occasion of paying
it to establish a stable financial image for Juan. Which should
probably include a permanent Colorado address for him, so
they don't start wondering.

OK—let's put our heads together and do this Tufts thing
right, for openers—just to take a nasty load off Juan. . . . Maybe
I should get in touch with them personally—or maybe I should
fly to Boston and check Juan in, as it were. Hang around for a
day or so while he registers, etc. . . . That sounds right to me,
but let's talk about it. (Letter to Mark Lipsky, 8/18/82)

As I read other letters to his accountant from that period, it
became clear that he was under serious financial stress at the
time. But he didn't want me to worry.

In a letter to Sandy in 1980, he wrote,

. . . and what the fuck makes you or anybody else think
I want to argue with lawyers about money for the rest of my
life? Why wouldn't I maybe just say "yes"—if you asked? For
anything fair. . . .

Why don't you just tell me what you want, or yes, what you
need to live decently without fouling both our lives with endless
haggling. (Juan has always been a separate issue to me. He is my
son and I love him and I suspect we sooner or later will get to
be good friends. . . . with no help from lawyers.)

I didn't see that letter until I started going through Hunter's
papers in 2006.

In another letter to a friend of his a couple of years later, he asks for a loan of $3,200 to pay my tuition, offering some original Steadman prints as collateral. In this letter he writes that he hopes I will remain ignorant of this loan.

Relationships are influenced so heavily by what we choose to remember and how we choose to interpret events. I think now that he cared very much, and that it did require a sacrifice, but it never occurred to me to look at the situation through any other lens than the one I was so used to using, the one that filtered out implicit acts of love and highlighted his selfishness and cruelty. Had it occurred to me, I would have begun to see that he loved me in a concrete and meaningful way.

Unfortunately, it took a long time for me to figure that out.

In the spring of 1982 it was time to graduate from boarding school. My grandmother Leah came from Florida, along with Sandy. My best friend Stevens Brosnihan and I had bought secondhand zoot suits for the ceremony, which was in a horse pasture along the irrigation ditch. My diploma was a rectangular piece of cowhide with the calligraphic text hand-lettered. I had invited Hunter and Laila, of course, and he assured me that he would come. But on the morning of the ceremony he wasn't there.

This was a recurring theme with Hunter and me. I knew not to expect anything from him, I knew he was extremely unreliable, yet I still felt disappointed when he let me down. I imagined that he had been asleep, or maybe he and Laila had had a fight, or maybe he just couldn't get himself together in time for the morning ceremony. I was sure that he hadn't forgotten, though, and I was sure he felt deeply guilty about it. But his guilt was no consolation. He had let me down at a crucial time, and the only conclusion I could draw was that it hadn't been sufficiently important to him to overcome his resistance, his inertia, his dislike of crowds of people, his exhaustion, or whatever. If the fights between him and my mother demonstrated his capacity for cruelty, this incident demonstrated the extent of his self-centeredness. We never talked about it, he never explained or apologized, I never asked why he hadn't come. Yet whenever I think of that day I am still angry at him, after forgiving him for so much else.

And yet that afternoon, after graduation, I went with a few of my friends from CRMS to Owl Farm. They were thrilled to meet Hunter. We shot guns, perhaps even set off a gasoline bomb. I had forgotten that until recently. We remember what we choose to remember.

That summer I traveled to Turkey with Stevens to see Sandy, who was living in the small town of Kas on the southern coast, and I met my mother's new boyfriend, William, who was twenty-six, while my mother was around forty-four.

If Don filled the role of an older brother and confidant, William was sibling and rival. He was a wonderful guy, friendly, kind, funny—but he was only a little older than I was. You don't have to be a psychologist to see the potential for disaster: I had a mother-son relationship with my mother based on biology, and she and William had a mother-son dynamic based on their age discrepancy. Sandy and I had a very close relationship bordering on the unhealthy. William had a new girlfriend and a rival for her affections. It was complicated. We would alternately have a lot of fun together and snip at each other over inconsequential things, just like siblings. On top of this, my mother was drinking regularly and heavily. I remember one night at a dinner party at a rooftop restaurant in Kas. There were maybe ten people there, and Sandy sat at the head of the table. She got drunk on wine

Hunter and Laila Nabulsi in the kitchen at Owl Farm, circa late 1990s

and began telling stories and delivering her opinions in a way that may have been entertaining to the others there, but which I found embarrassing and distasteful. Stevens and I left early, disgusted. We left a few days later to do some touring of Turkey on our own while Sandy and William remained in Kas.

At the end of that summer, before I started college, I went to Owl Farm to spend a week or so with Hunter. He was in the middle of writing *The Curse of Lono* and was having a rough time with it. He asked me to read the first chapter and wanted my opinion. That was a tricky thing, to give him my opinion on his writing. I knew well his capacity for anger and how he could effortlessly reduce an opponent to tears with a few expertly chosen words. Yet I wanted to be honest. I didn't want to be another sycophant, and there were many by that time, feeding him cheap praise. So I gave him my thoughts, carefully, erring on the side of praise, but not exclusively. He seemed to take it well, no explosions of rage or scorching wrath. He didn't take my advice at the time, but neither did he take offense. That was a big deal, when I think of it now. His writing was the most important thing in the world to him, and he asked me my opinion.

We also did some shooting, cleaned guns, watched some Bogart movies, and one day went motorcycling. He still had a dirt bike then, he borrowed another one for me from his best friend, Oliver Treibick, and the two of us went for a long ride into the hills.

We wound up into the mountains and finally emerged on a hilltop overlooking the Woody Creek Valley. I remember sitting there on our motorcycles, side by side, commenting on the extraordinary view. At last, my father and I were spending time together, just the two of us, riding motorcycles in the hills, doing what guys do. We didn't have many of these moments, so when they happened, they carried a lot of weight. Sure, it was partly a fantasy, both of us acting as if all the horrible things had never happened, but there we were, together.

Two days later I left for college, for Tufts University in Boston.

SIX

INDEPENDENCE: AGES 18 TO 24

Tufts—The cub reporter—Priorities—Rolling Stone—
Al-Anon in earnest—The letters—A year abroad—The
correspondent's coat—Graduation with honors

HST TIMELINE

1983 *The Curse of Lono* published *Fear and Loathing in Las Vegas*
      published in Finland.
      Hunter spends a few months each year up until 1987 in the
      Florida Keys working on *The Silk Road,* a novel about the
      Mariel Boatlift.
1984 Meets the Mitchell brothers, works as night manager of
      O'Farrell Theatre in San Francisco.
1985 Still in San Francisco.
1987 *Fear and Loathing in Las Vegas* published in Spain and Germany.
1988 *Generation of Swine* published, a compilation of columns for
      the *San Francisco Examiner. Fear and Loathing in Las Vegas*
      published in France and Denmark.

A S I WAS GETTING on the plane in Aspen to fly to Boston, Hunter gave me a letter. He told me to read it once I
was in-flight.

Sept 1 '82

Dear Juan

Okay. You're off. And things seem generally under control—
on your end, anyway. I am still juggling madness on this end, +
I've never even heard a rumor that the end might be in sight.

It's a queer life for sure—but at least it keeps me in shape,
more or less.

Here are three valid $50 checks, which should keep you
solvent at least long enough to settle in + get a fix on things.
Use them to open your own bank account in Boston.

Also, <u>call me tonight </u>to confirm your safe arrival. <u>Don't
forget to do this.</u> Tonight.

The sheepskin jacket is a present from Laila. Boston is cold
in the winter.

I'll call Dick + Doris [Goodwin] + Mike Barnicle at the
Globe, to say you'll be stopping by sometime soon, to say hello,
etc.

- ooo -

Call your advisor from the Denver airport + say you'll be late
for dinner—but you'll try to make it + you'd like to meet him
tonight. Also, ask him the best way to get from the airport to
Tufts ASAP. . . . and tell him you're very concerned that your
application for the school newspaper didn't get there on time.
Can he help you straighten out the confusion?

He can. But you'll have to get serious about it right away. Gall
is a basic tool of journalism, which is a rude business at best.

- ooo -

And so much for advice + logistics. I'm not worried about
you—but I am interested, and I'll want to know what's
happening. Send me your phone number and a P.O. address.
Let's talk on the phone as often as you feel like it—especially for

the first few weeks, which will almost certainly be nervous. Or maybe not. But if they are, don't worry. The Glum Reaper will be hanging around, but to hell with him. We have dealt with the bugger before + we know the one thing he can't handle is a bedrock sense of humor.

So remember the 44 "Naked + Alone . . ." books. All you have to do is write the first two. I'll handle it after that, + we will both get obscenely rich. Take my word for it. Why fool around with tangents, like all the others? Your future is already assured. All you need is a typewriter + a few reams of paper.

- ooo -

I'm glad you came home for a while, + I wish it could have been longer. I had a good time—and as always, was proud of you. Very few seekers go out in the world as well-armed as you are.

I'll keep after [Paul] Rubin for the $1000 he owes you for technical work. He says he has a fat job for you next summer— but so do I, and mine is a lot fatter. 44 books, rich + famous by 21. No problem.

Even Oliver was impressed with the way you handled his motorcycle, and I will carry the scars of our ride forever. Thank god for aloe.

And sleep. We didn't get much of that, but your work on the LONO book was far more valuable than a simple thing like sleep. We didn't <u>cure</u> the Blue Arm, but we caught it just in time to avert a serious problem.

But not entirely. I still have a lot of real work to do—+ I'll get on it today; and maybe try that idea of a 12-day run, like Georges Simenon. Two more weeks are about all I can spend on LONO. After that, it's down to Florida for the Silk Road— which will be critical to both of our futures. It will live or die on the dialogue—+ for that I will have to get re-acquainted with my own sense of humor. Mean dullards tend to write mean, dull dialogue.

- ooo -

Anyway, I'll figure on seeing you for Xmas, if not before that. We had a wonderful time with Davison + his family last year, + hopefully we can do it again—either here or in Florida, depending on my Silk Road schedule. . . . So let's keep this in mind + plan for it.

We still have a ways to go before we can act like good friends + yell at each other without worrying about what it all means. . . . But we're doing pretty well, considering the small amount of time we've really put into it.

You're a good person, and I love you for that as much as because you're my son.

Or because you're about to be rich + pay my expenses forever. With my wisdom + your talent, our bets are covered from the start. By 1984 we'll be making $44,000 a month, and even Jimmy [Buffett] will be standing in line to get your autograph.

Let's stop looking at this college gig as a foolish expense + start seeing it as an avenue to big money: a fine investment, with huge returns in the offing. Right? Yes. Let's do it. Love, H.

Sometimes apparently ordinary events or objects encapsulate vast realities. This letter is one. What is perhaps most remarkable is that I had completely forgotten about this letter until I rediscovered it during my research for this book. It is the letter I had been waiting for my whole life, a promise of an engaged father who gives advice, gives encouragement, promises adventure, affirms the good times, and talks of getting together soon. All of a sudden I had a father again. How could I have forgotten this letter?

However, we moved too fast toward a kind of intimacy that

we both wished for but which did not yet exist. I took him at his word, plunged in and sent him a letter expressing my loneliness, sadness, homesickness, and depression. I wasn't going to leave Tufts and retreat to Aspen this time, but it wasn't an easy transition. I was exceedingly lonely, I didn't know anyone and still didn't know how to talk to strangers. Once again, after three years of being a part of a small and intimate community at CRMS, I was on my own.

I arrived in Boston, and like Concord three years earlier, it was foreign. It was a big city—I had never lived in a city. The people were different, the streets were different, and their accents were different. Tufts is an island of wealthy academia in the middle of a run-down neighborhood on the border of Medford and Somerville, two towns that were absorbed into metropolitan Boston a long time ago. I looked like a fourteen-year-old Native American boy with hair down to my shoulders and bangs that hid my eyes. This time I was fortunate to have a great roommate, Peter. He came from an upper-class family on Long Island, had attended St. Paul's Academy before coming to Tufts, wore chinos and oxford shirts rolled up to the elbows, and competed on the sailing team. He made me feel very welcome, though we could not have been more different. He also had the exceptional decency that year to let me use his car many nights, an old Volvo 240 sedan, so I could go on long drives around the city. Peter made a lonely, difficult year bearable. I hope life has been good to you, Peter, wherever you are.

During the freshman orientation there was a social event in our dormitory where all the freshmen milled about, ate cookies, and drank pop. I dreaded that event, though I went, and sat by myself the entire time. I didn't know what to say.

Some nights—or more accurately some mornings—Hunter would call. It might be two or three a.m., early by Hunter's standards and time zone, but the very middle of the night for me. I would stagger out of bed and grab the receiver, and then go out into the hall to avoid waking my roommate. Mostly we would talk about nothing in particular—politics, Owl Farm, his current project. He would ask how things were going and I would give him a brief update. Sometimes we had business to discuss, such as the tuition payment. Sometimes I would slump to the floor and hold the phone to my ear with my eyes closed, dead tired, just wanting to go to sleep but grateful to hear Hunter's voice and grateful for his reaching out to me. I see now he wasn't calling to chat. We didn't really have that kind of relationship yet. He was calling to find out how I was doing. The letters hadn't worked as a medium, instead creating more confusion than clarity on both sides, so he called to check up on me in his indirect way, feeling things out from my tone of voice, what I did or did not mention.

His friend Oliver had a brother who lived just outside of Boston. Oliver got in touch with his brother and asked him to keep an eye on me. Three or four times I went to their house on weekends. It was in a Boston suburb, but heavily wooded and with plenty of space between the houses, more like ranchettes than suburban tracts, except Massachusetts doesn't have ranches or ranchettes. I would walk in the woods, or read, or talk with Oliver's brother, who was a doctor. I remember one day while he was working in the garage I asked him questions about cocaine and other drugs, how they worked on the brain, what exactly was dangerous about them. He seemed happy to answer and I was grateful to be with people who had some connection to my roots, rather than spending another weekend on campus alone.

In the first few weeks of school I took Hunter's advice and went down to the office of *The Tufts Observer*. I had no experience as a reporter at all, since my boarding school did not have a newspaper. They gave me an assignment to cover the meeting of the student government. That evening I walked over to the room where the student government officials were gathered and listened to them talk, and talk, and talk. There was the recitation of the meeting minutes, the motions, the votes, the agenda, and long discussions of extraordinarily dull topics. I had my pen and notebook, but I could barely stay awake, much less take meaningful notes. The meeting went on for hours. After it was over I was supposed to write a short article on the proceedings, but I couldn't think of a single thing to write. I never turned in that assignment and put an end to my journalistic career—with no regrets.

I wonder where the notion to work for the student paper came from. I don't remember having any strong interest in being a journalist, and I can't imagine Hunter actually encouraging me to take up a profession that he has so frequently denigrated, yet Hunter and I had obviously talked about it before I left for Tufts. There was also the burden of having to be good at it. I was Hunter Thompson's son, after all, and much would be expected of me—by Hunter, by myself, and by others. I was not ready for that kind of pressure. I had always steered away from writing as a profession because I knew well how difficult it was to make a living as a freelance writer, but also because I didn't want to try and fail at it. I felt an actual terror at the thought of venturing into Hunter's world professionally, because the stakes were so high personally; he might be disappointed, I might be disappointed. It seemed better not even to consider the same profession.

And yet, in a letter I wrote to Hunter shortly after I arrived at Tufts, I brought up the idea of joining the college paper as though it was something I very much wanted to do. I even wrote that I wanted to become the editor of the paper. Why would I write Hunter such a thing, given my ambivalence about pursuing writing, and journalism in particular? I must have been trying to impress him, to get my father's approval by seeking success in his profession. How foolish. How unnecessary. How poignant. Hunter never encouraged me to be a writer. Instead, most often he encouraged me to develop my skills as a computer hacker. Back when the personal computer was just developing, even before the IBM PC, Apple II, the Commodore 64, and the Radio Shack TRS-80, back when the chip was a 4Mhz Z-80 processor and the language a primitive thing called TINY-BASIC, I had been hounding Hunter to purchase a kit computer. He would counter with two questions: How would it help him, and would I in turn promise to devote myself to figuring out how to break into a banking computer and make us rich? I couldn't answer the former and couldn't agree to the latter, so I had to wait a few more years to buy a TRS-80 myself.

To cope with my loneliness at Tufts, I took long walks between classes through the neighborhoods around the school, and later throughout Boston. On weekends I would often walk down Massachusetts Avenue to Harvard Square where I would visit bookstores, see a movie, or just wander through the streets. At night I would plot out a destination on the city map, maybe the Charles River, maybe Harvard Square again, maybe somewhere in downtown Boston, and walk there and back, sometimes a journey of five or six hours through dubious neighborhoods. Other nights I would borrow my roommate's car and drive out to Nahant, a tiny island just south of Marblehead that is connected to the mainland by a thread of a sandbar. At the tip of the island is the Northeastern University Marine Science Center. I would walk over the dunes and out onto the jagged boulders at the water's edge, where I could see the lights of Boston about five miles away and watch the waves crash against the rocks. Other nights I would climb up the fire escape on one of the tall old buildings on campus to a little platform just below the roof. It was about five stories, and the campus was built on a hill, so from my perch I had a sweeping view of nighttime Boston.

Standing on the rocks at Nahant, or sitting on that platform, I had solitude, but not loneliness. I had the pleasure of my company, though I did dream, in a vague romantic way, of sitting there with a beautiful young woman. The night was a thick, warm, and intimate cloak that hid and protected me. At those times I imagined myself a brooding, deeply sensitive soul separated from his peers by a deeper understanding of life.

If the night was a cloak in which I could hide, daytime was nakedness and shame. I felt exposed, seen, and judged by everyone around me. I could not walk down a sidewalk or a street with other people without a profound sense of awkward self consciousness. If I had solitude at night, I had raw loneliness by day, emphasized, or perhaps made possible, by the presence of all the people around me with whom I could not connect, not because I was aloof and made of a finer stuff, but because I didn't know how. The time during class was manageable because there was no expectation of socializing. It was the time between classes, or during meals, when people talk to each other, that my isolation was so excruciatingly obvious to me.

Mealtime at the dormitory was the worst. All those people, all that talk, all those connections around me in which I had no part. It was unbearable to eat alone with no distraction. I would eat as fast as possible and still the meal seemed to take hours. I solved this problem by getting a subscription to *The Boston Globe* and reading the paper during meals, just as I had read Tolkien at Concord Academy a few years earlier.

It was in this state of mind that I wrote this letter to Hunter, full of disdain for the people around me, a disdain and arrogance born out of loneliness and fear.

Sept 4th, 1982

Hunter,

Yes—naked and alone in Boston. How baffling this is. "I'm not like the others!" The glum reaper is devious this time. He hides outside the window, the tip of his scythe barely visible. Thankfully, he doesn't show his miserable, despairing form, but I know he's there. Other times he's not so subtle. He and I walk side by side, completely alone, so close I can smell the tears, the utter hopelessness of this endeavor. He shows me memories, vivid nostalgia, better times. It's deadly, and very painful. And then, he retreats, I am reprieved, he never lets me forget he is there, though. Devious, insidious. I feel the best I've felt since I've been here. As I write this, light glints off the blade of that scythe, moves a bit farther out . . . It's true, I'm not like the others. I'm quiet, "weird," solitary. What can I say? I'm sure there are, among Tufts' 5000 students, at least a hundred people with whom I can make friends, but they are as invisible as I. The social codes are different, distinctly preppy, fraternity-sorority, hip, flip, fast-and-cute, nauseating, and artificial. I have no doubt that the majority of these people are interesting, likeable, intelligent people. Unfortunately, they've been taught not to show it. The problem lies in socializing. When these people socialize, they don a common "mask." They talk a certain way (hip, flip) act a certain way, do certain things, all of which have been defined as socially acceptable. By acting in such a way, one makes "friends." With time, friends use their masks less and less, and a true, deep friendship results. But the mask is so cheap, and repulsive! I don't want to use it, so I take the alternative (which is not necessarily best) and retreat, becoming quiet and "unsociable," waiting to meet someone like me. Lonelier. The price of principles. The price of a progressive, Aspen, western education. The Community School. I'd do it a thousand times over.

Tried calling you tonight—no answer. Play? You're right about the sense of humor. The Ultimate Weapon. Unfortunately, humor seems so far away when I most need it. I've made a sign, "Naked and Alone" . . . which I'm putting on the wall. Perhaps Tufts isn't the place for me, perhaps the east isn't the place for me. Nevertheless, I'll definitely plan to stay a year here, to make a fair judgment. No Concord fiasco, I'm more sensible than that. Yeah, it's easy to say that behind "His" back, but when he's beside me, it's hard.

My roommate wears the mask. The other night he took it off (why?) and was very nice. A pleasant person and worthwhile roommate. The next morning, and ever since, he's had it on. The room is looking better. Once I get my boxes it will be quite nice, I think. Now, I could stick it out. Tomorrow, when HE comes, I won't be very sure. Don't worry, I'll survive.

By the way, this newspaper, The Tufts Observer, needs a good reporter. More importantly, it needs a good editor. Too ambitious? We'll see . . . If this is one of the top 5 college papers, I couldn't bear to see the worst. It needs work. So, Monday or Tuesday I'll get on the staff, get my foot in the door, so to speak. I hope they aren't stodgy, intellectual, fraternity snobs running the paper. They may well be.

My phone number is: 617 628 2043

Please call anytime. I really enjoyed your letter, thank you, it helped. Get some work done. I'll be working hard here. Fear is in the air. These people would rather be at Harvard. Old Harvard. These people will be running this country. Not me, I'm not like the others, I won't be. Never!

Can I maintain such a claim in the face of such as HE? I'll make friends, slowly, as is my nature. Slow but steady. I'll send for some literature on Reed College in Oregon. Just look. A year here may be long enough, or just the beginning. Remind me, Keep me honest, my objectivity can be easily lost here.

Enough!

I love you, Dad.

Juan

When I found this letter to Hunter in the archive, I also found his notes that he had scrawled on the letter:

Yeah. "they'll (sic) all gay like me—why won't they admit it?"

Jesus. What hath Sandy wrought?

No college will cure this problem—only postpone it, for $1500 a month.

That would pay the mortgage on the Owl Farm.

I have already paid $5000. Another $1000 due on Oct. 1st.

Can Sandy take me back to court if I don't pay?

So what? He'll be in the Village by then.

A few weeks later Hunter replied with a rambling, confused letter in which he recounted a story about the last time he received such a letter in which a friend of his informed him that he was gay and was going to New York City "to be with his people."

Hunter wrote that their friendship petered out after a few get-togethers, not because of Hunter's hostility to gays, but because they now had different interests and social circles. He finished the letter with this:

> . . . there is a knotty kind of intensity in your message that was exceeded only by its obscurity. So I figured I'd just skrike out in the fog and see what came of it. None of my doctorates gave me wisdom in areas like these—but I sense something heavier than just college on your mind and I think I should know what it is. Tell me.

I had written him two long letters explaining how lonely and unhappy I was and his reaction was to tell me I wasn't being clear and to state the real problem. I had asked my father, who in his previous letter had been so supportive and welcoming of communication, for help or understanding, and now he was no help at all. In fact, his letter brought up uncomfortable questions: Did my father think I was gay? Was he saying that we would drift apart if I were? What was he trying to say? Did he understand me at all? Clearly he could not help me.

That first letter from Hunter was beautiful wishful thinking. He wanted to believe we had that kind of relationship, as did I. We wanted to believe we could start over from that moment and he could be the father he and I both wanted him to be. My letters to him exploded that illusion, and now I see he had no idea how to handle this kind of appeal from me. He could give practical advice; if I had asked him for help getting a job, getting a car, getting an interview for an article in the student paper, that he could have handled. But a cry of loneliness in the darkness, that he could not handle.

What it showed most clearly is that we did not know each other, though we badly wanted to, and as a result he could not help me at a time when I very much needed his help. He simply did not understand. We did not have the history, the thousands of hours of shared time and experience over years that we could draw on for understanding each other. I wanted his understanding, acceptance, and reassurance. I wanted him to tell me that he loved me, that I was going to be okay, that I was going through a rough time but that I would come out of it. I wanted to hear that I would find my people here just as I had at CRMS, and that I would find a woman to love and who would love me for who I was, a shy, introspective, book-loving, sensitive, and insecure young man. I wanted him to tell me to believe in myself, because I was a Thompson and I was his son, and I would thrive in my own way and in my own time. He wanted a concrete problem to solve or at least react to, something that he could relate to. We were very different people.

I kept writing letters, but not to Hunter. We talked now and then, but not about my unhappiness. As Hunter wrote in that first letter, "We still have a ways to go before we can act like good friends. . . ." This series of letters had made it clear just how far we still had to go.

I stayed at Tufts that year, but I never did find my people. I continued my solitary walks all that year, nights and weekends, getting home at two or three a.m. Those walks helped keep me sane.

Some friends from CRMS came to visit me at Tufts throughout the year. These visits were spots of color in a gray time, but also a reminder of what I did not have. When they left, I felt my loneliness more sharply than ever.

I had no intention of returning to Tufts the following year.

I considered Bennington College where Stevens was going, but Hunter nixed that idea both because it was even more expensive than Tufts, and because he said that if I was going to go to college and he was going to pay for it, it had better be a decent school, not, to paraphrase Hunter, some overpriced day care center for self-indulgent artists manqués. So we were at a stalemate. When the school year was over, I headed to New York City for a summer internship at *Rolling Stone* magazine. That, at least, was something Hunter could help me with. That and the use of a studio apartment in the West Village for fifty dollars a month, courtesy of Judy Belushi, widow of John Belushi, who was a good friend of Hunter's before his death. It was a very comfortable way to experience New York City for the first time.

I worked at *Rolling Stone* as an editorial intern, which meant that I was an all-purpose gofer. I would do research for editors, file photos for the photo department, and occasionally run down to a street vendor for a hot dog for Jann Wenner, the editor and publisher. I was paid around seven dollars an hour, but with my fifty-dollar rent, no car, and no expensive vices, it was sufficient. The work was not memorable. Its greatest value was to observe the life of magazine editors and staff writers, and to realize that it was not for me.

That summer Laila and Hunter were on their final descent. Laila had discovered Al-Anon and realized that much of Hunter's behavior was attributable to alcoholism. I had conversations with her on the phone, discussing whether Hunter would go to a treatment center, whether he would stay, and what her options were. She ended up giving him an ultimatum: either he went to a treatment center or she would leave. Hunter actually did go to the treatment center in Florida for a few days, but then rebelled and escaped with the help of a friend. Laila left him for good shortly thereafter. That was the beginning of a long dialogue over the years between Laila and me about Hunter as an alcoholic, which put Hunter's behavior, and mine, into a context that I could start to understand.

THE HIGHLIGHT of that summer was meeting Susannah, a beautiful twenty-six-year-old editorial assistant at *Rolling Stone.* She was permanent staff and she got to write a couple of short items in the magazine now and then, but was essentially a secretary to the editors. She and I started dating, and at the end of the summer she quit *Rolling Stone,* I finished my internship, and since I had not applied to a college besides Bennington, which Hunter had vetoed with prejudice, we headed south to Florida to join my mother and William on her new thirty-seven-foot sailboat, on which they lived. We had some vague plans about going to India, or maybe Europe.

Susannah was an answer to my prayers. She was smart, funny, artsy, sarcastic, loved to read, and she liked me as I was, bowl cut and all. She became my person, and New York City transformed from a large and lonely place to an adventure. She was my mentor/lover. She introduced me to art movies—I saw *Last Tango in Paris* and Godard's *Breathless* at a little theater in the Village. She told me about new bands, and we talked about books. I loved her and was devoted to her. We weren't equals—I was her naïve puppy dog and her pupil—but I was fine with this arrangement. I had a real girlfriend. I was loved, and I wasn't alone.

The Turkey trip had been tense, but this trip to Florida could have been the basis for a Tennessee Williams play. Start with a forty-five-year-old woman and her handsome twenty-seven-year-old husband (they had gotten married a year earlier). Add her twenty-year-old son with whom she has had an unusually close relationship, and his attractive twenty-six-year-old girlfriend, who happened to be almost the same age as the mother's husband. Add a heap of tension between Susannah and the mother, put them all on a small boat for two months, add heat and my mother's fondness for wine at the time, and wait for the fireworks to start.

And they did. After two months everyone was angry at everyone else, and Susannah and I fled the boat and went to Aspen. I had nowhere else to go, and Susannah came with me. In retrospect I think, Why would she want to go to Aspen with a twenty-year-old boy? Maybe because she didn't know what the hell she was doing and she didn't have a better idea. Like me.

But I was very happy to have her along. I had my person and she had me, so we didn't each feel so terribly alone. We bummed along in Aspen for a year. I got a job at the Explore bookstore and Susannah got a job as an executive secretary. We had planned to house-sit at Owl Farm while Hunter was in the Florida Keys for the winter, but when we arrived Hunter was not ready. First, we stayed in a friend's basement in Basalt, about fifteen miles from Aspen, and then we moved to a tiny apartment belonging to another friend. This went on for several more months, Hunter always on the verge, never quite ready to leave. Eventually it became clear he wasn't leaving at all and we found a longer-term house-sitting situation. We ended up staying in a lovely house in Old Snowmass twenty miles outside of Aspen, in a quiet valley on several acres of land, right next to the river. We stayed there the spring and the first part of the summer until we moved to Boulder. On weekends I would take long walks up onto the mesas, or hikes up into the mountains, with Lolita, the Australian sheepdog we were taking care of. It was so quiet, so calm, and so beautiful in that valley that it made up for all the craziness leading up to it.

I spent the time in Aspen working at the local bookstore and then as a maintenance man for a property management company. It only took a few months of this to realize that I had to get back to college as soon as possible, that this was no way to live. There I was, retreating to Aspen after one year of college, with no solid skills and, more important, no reason to be there except that I had nowhere else to go. This was life without a plan or a goal, and I couldn't bear it. I didn't know exactly what I wanted to do, but I knew I couldn't stay in Aspen and that I had to get back in school.

Susannah and I had had dinner one night with Hunter at the Holiday Inn, which was at the base of Buttermilk, on the highway on the way into Aspen. After dinner we drove back to Owl Farm to pick up our car and head home. We stood in the living room by the front door, and while we were talking Hunter glanced at the bookshelves by the door and noticed that several books were missing. He got angry and though he wouldn't accuse me directly, it was clear that he suspected us of taking the books. I took the logical approach: I didn't take the books, I didn't know who had, and there was nothing more to say. However, he would not drop the subject. In an angry tone he told us how he hated being looted, as if dwelling on the topic would somehow dislodge more information from us. I didn't know what more to say. I was uncomfortable and ready to leave. Susannah took a different approach. She became defiant and emphatically denied taking any books. He and Susannah stared at each other, then Hunter backed down and said something about how sometimes he just had to yell. She said, "Can I yell too?" Then Hunter smiled, and hugged her, and said that sometimes we have to go through these things. I saw in that exchange that Hunter respected strength, and that sometimes, but not always, a fierce response would settle him down. But sometimes, it would spur him on to greater wrath. I could never be sure. My father was a warrior, not a philosopher.

THAT WHOLE YEAR seems unreal and disconnected. Susannah and I were not living toward something, we had no intention of ever getting married or having children, we were together almost by accident, like two survivors on a raft taking solace in each other's company, drifting with the current.

The best thing that came out of that year was a strong desire to get back in school. I remember standing in the bookstore where I worked, surrounded by all that creativity, all that knowledge, those myriad worlds of experiences, and deciding that I had to get back in college and out of Aspen. I applied to the University of Colorado. I was a shoo-in and in-state tuition was affordable. Hunter agreed to continue to pay for school.

Susannah had no attachment to Aspen, and so that summer we drove over to Boulder, where I would be starting school in a couple of months, and found an apartment downtown on Pine Street. In August we moved what few possessions we had and started our lives there.

Susannah got a job working for the city or county of Boulder, I can't recall which, while I started school as a sophomore, which meant that I was exempt from all of the required socializing with freshmen students, and that I could live off-campus. I was grateful for this, but it also meant that I had no real connections at school. I would show up for my classes and head home, talking to almost no one, making no friends. But Susannah was my friend,

I didn't need any others. I have heard the phrase "playing house," and that's what we were doing: playing house. I was enjoying it, not knowing any better. We had a wonderful apartment, we had a routine, and I had a best friend in Susannah.

That Thanksgiving Hunter called and said he was in Denver and proposed that we get together. This was short notice, but Susannah and I had no other plans, so we agreed. We considered having dinner at our apartment, but we had only two chairs, so we decided it would be better to go to a restaurant.

For the first and last time in my life, Hunter came to my home. Thanksgiving night Hunter and Maria, his new assistant and lover, came to Boulder. I remember it was dark and we came outside to meet them at the curb. This was the first time I met Maria. She was petite, as Hunter's women tended to be, and young, beautiful, and very intelligent. They always were. My second impression was of her kindness and sincerity. They came inside for a bit and then we went to the restaurant in the Hilton for Thanksgiving dinner, just the four of us in a practically abandoned dining room. It was a strangely stereotypical scene: my father and his beautiful girlfriend came to visit his son and his girlfriend at college, except his girlfriend was younger than mine. Hunter asked Susannah to pick the wine. We had a quiet and polite conversation with no yelling or embarrassing scenes. The only hints that this was not a normal family were Maria's age, twenty-three, and the fact that she was assisting him with his article on the notorious Mitchell Brothers and their O'Farrell Theatre, a large and upscale strip club in San Francisco. That, and the number of whiskeys Hunter finished off during and after dinner. On the way home we stopped at Liquor Mart for a big bottle of Chivas, and when we parted at the curb at our apartment, Hunter handed Susannah an empty whiskey bottle to dispose of. In Hunter's world, this was normal, like asking someone to throw away an empty Starbucks cup.

One of the most difficult paradoxes in Hunter's character was the presence of both a strong, genuine caring for others, and a profound self-centeredness. One time at Owl Farm, I was talking with Maria about some issue with the computer. Hunter was in the kitchen at the counter, in his usual post-waking ritual of reading the paper, watching a game, and nibbling on breakfast. At one point Maria and I went into the office where the computer was located so I could show her something. We were in the office for ten or fifteen minutes when suddenly the lights went out and the computer went dark. It lasted maybe fifteen seconds, and then the power came on again. I assumed it was a power grid problem. After all, Owl Farm is in the country and power outages weren't unusual. Maria said to me, "He wants us back in the kitchen." It took me a few seconds to comprehend what she meant. What she seemed to be saying was that Hunter had turned off the power in that part of the house to flush us out. She explained to me that Hunter could not bear to not be the center of attention, and that he had reached the limits of his patience.

We walked back into the kitchen and Hunter was still there in his chair as if nothing had happened, yet he didn't look entirely innocent. He looked as if he were trying to appear absorbed in the newspaper. Maria confronted him with something like, "That was very childish, Hunter." He didn't respond, yet he didn't deny it either, as though now that he had gotten what he wanted he was going to continue his morning uninterrupted. Hunter often quoted in his writing a bit of political wisdom, "Never apologize, never explain," and that is precisely what he did that day. I think he was also jealous of any friendship between Maria and me. I understood after that incident that my father was in some ways like a small child who could not imagine that the world did not center on him alone.

Hunter was on his best behavior when I was around. Things were much worse when I was not around. To those poor suffering saints, or masochists, who subjected themselves to Hunter daily for years, and sometimes decades as in Deborah's case, Hunter could be a monster. I rarely saw these excoriations, and only occasionally heard about them. To be with Hunter day after day, while he was flogging himself, flaying himself with guilt, shame, and fear, trying to provoke within himself the energy, no matter how vile and poisonous its source, to complete whatever assignment was in front of him, was to witness something truly terrible. To see him turn his pent-up frustration against himself was in some ways the most painful, because he was relentless and complete in his self-degradation and despair. More often, though, he turned it outward, against those around him. Vicious, blistering verbal or written attacks. He was always a physically powerful man, even into his sixties, but it wasn't physical violence that you had to worry about, it was the verbal attack. Hunter could be a southern gentleman, particularly with beautiful young women whom he had recently met and was trying to seduce. With interviewers he could be similarly charming, but with those who knew him best, who lived with him day after day, he was always brilliant, often monstrous, sometimes tender and funny, occasionally supportive, but never gentlemanly. There is a reason that no woman lasted more than four or five years, and as time passed, closer to two—he was impossible to live with. Over time he just wore his women out.

I find that I mark time in Hunter's life according to the significant women in his life. First there was Laila. She had a long run, about six years. Then there was Maria, who made it for four or five years. Following her was Terry, who made it for a couple of years, then Nicole, for another couple of years. Then, one after another, there was Madeline, Heidi, and Anita, whom he married a little more than a year before his death. There were others, of course, between and during, I have no idea how many. They were almost always very young, in their twenties. At first they were somewhat older than me. Laila was like an older sister, since I was sixteen and she was maybe twenty-four. Maria was much closer to my age, a year or two older, and by the time Nicole came into his life, I was older than her at thirty-two while she was probably twenty-five. Hunter and I grew older, yet his women stayed about the same age.

I learned a lot about Hunter through his women, either from them directly or from watching the growth, maturity, and demise of the relationships. They began hopefully. I would meet them for the first time at Owl Farm, and they would have heard much about me. I knew nothing about them. They were anxious to please, and I was wary and skeptical. I wanted to understand who this woman was, and why she was here. Was she worthy of my father, and worthy of living at Owl Farm? However, Hunter didn't ask me what I thought. He had his own reasons, and he wasn't interested in my opinions on his women. After the new woman and I had negotiated the initial awkwardness and we had accepted each other, there arose a kind of unspoken collaboration between us, and alliance of understanding, particularly with Laila, Maria, and Nicole, the women he loved most deeply.

There was that initial phase of hopefulness in which the love between them was so evident. Hunter glowed with this calm joy. They were like two teenagers. I came to understand that Hunter was a hopeless romantic. He loved to fall in love, to be in love. This was a part of his life that he did not share with me, but from his letters I can see what a dedicated suitor he was. Romantic letters, faxes, notes, late-night rendezvous, road trips, flights to New York, L.A., or some exotic place, and the complete attention of a very charismatic, famous (in some circles anyway) older man, must have made a powerful impression on young women.

I realize now that it was usually, maybe always, his girlfriends, and later Deb, who orchestrated his family gatherings such as that Thanksgiving in Boulder. It's not that Hunter didn't want to see his family, it was that he was incapable of initiating it.

It was the same, I am sure, when Hunter and Laila spent Christmas with Hunter's brother Davison and his family in Ohio several years earlier. No doubt Hunter had been meaning to reach out, feeling guilty after every Christmas, Thanksgiving, and birthday that he failed to contact his family, and yet he never seemed able to translate that guilt into action. It was up to the new woman in his life to actually make it happen.

Perhaps I knew this deep down, but it didn't matter. Whatever the reason for his visit that Thanksgiving in 1984, I was glad to see him.

The following March was my twenty-first birthday and Hunter had a surprise in mind. He was living in Sausalito with Maria at the time and spending a lot of time at the O'Farrell Theatre, where he had become the honorary night manager. What he actually did in that capacity he never did explain. He invited Susannah and me out for a weekend. I much later found out that the vice president and general manager of the theater, Jeff Armstrong, had arranged and paid for the entire weekend at Hunter's request. When we arrived, we picked up a red convertible rental that I'm sure Hunter picked out for us. We stayed at the downtown Marriott high above San Francisco. Our room was large and had a balcony. Best of all, the city was sunny and warm.

We drove to Sausalito to see Hunter and Maria. I remember it was on the side of a steep hill, not far from the bay. It was a small house stacked in among lots of other small houses that crowded the steep hillside by the water. The roads were narrow and curvy and there were no driveways. Their house, or cottage actually, had a wall of windows and a big deck that looked out over the bay.

That night Hunter took us to his office, just like any father might do, except in this case it was the O'Farrell Theatre. His "office" was a large room on the second floor with windows that overlooked the street, and resembled a recreation room from the basement of a suburban home, with a pool table in the middle of the room, black leather couches around the walls, and a variety of art and trophies. There was probably a bar as well, but I was aggressively opposed to alcohol at the time, so I took no notice. There was a tiny office off to the side with a couple of 1950s metal desks, two small windows and fake wood paneling that reminded me of a trailer, but the rec room was clearly the heart of the operation. This is where Hunter and the Mitchell Brothers held court, surrounded by beautiful women.

He told us about the various rooms in the theater. There was the movie theater that showed porn flicks, the New York Live stage show, the Ultra Room, and the Kopenhagen Room. He said one room involved naked women, a dark room, and customers with flashlights, while another of the rooms had a live peep show. The whole scene was, of course, titillating and awkward for me, and became more so when Hunter led Susannah and me through the dancers' dressing room to the sound and light booth over-looking the New York Live Stage. I was intensely aware of walk-ing by beautiful, partly or wholly naked women standing and chatting in front of their lockers, like guys in a locker room, com-pletely unconcerned by our presence. I, of course, averted my

eyes and acted casual, as if I were walking down an aisle at Target.
The show was in full swing. In the booth, standing next to the
lighting technician, we could see a woman stripping onstage to
music, and at the end of the performance, disappearing offstage
and reappearing a few minutes later in the audience dressed in
lingerie. Hunter explained that they were providing lap dances,
leaving the details to my imagination.

When I think back on it now, I wonder what Hunter was up
to. He knew, of course, that it would be awkward for me, especially with Susannah there, and I think he wanted to see how
she would react. I can imagine that it was always interesting to
bring a self-proclaimed feminist to the O'Farrell and watch her
reaction. Sometimes it was genuine curiosity that motivated his
probing, and sometimes it was just the prankster at work.

I realize now that for all his courage and public madness and
the power of his words, Hunter was very circumspect when it
came to matters of the heart. In the national media he called
Nixon "a predatory shyster . . . full of claws and bleeding string-
warts," but when it came to those he loved, he would not speak
directly. Instead, he would observe and sense. After the final separation of my parents, the divorce proceedings began, and the
lawyers got involved. It is remarkable now, reading notes between
him and Sandy in 1977 and 1978, before that final separation, to
see how hard they both were trying to overcome their differences,
to be patient, to reassure each other that the love and willingness
to succeed as a family was there. But it was not sufficient to overcome the history and the anger and the habits that had led them
to separation in the first place, and once they decided to give it
up for good, it got ugly. Hunter realized that the disintegration
of our family was going to be hard for me.

But we never talked about it. He never told me that this was going to be hard, or that if I started to feel like my life was coming apart, that was normal. He could have said a lot of things that many fathers these days, trained in the modern methods of clear communication by their therapists, might say. We could have talked it through, as I would with my son now. But that was not his way, as it is not my son's way. My son doesn't want to necessarily talk about his hurts. I want to have an open discussion, make sure we are communicating unambiguously and explicitly, but that is not his way. He has a low tolerance for discussing highly personal matters in such a blunt and objective way, as if the intensity of the topic is too much for him to endure for more than a couple of minutes at most, as if he can see more clearly by looking indirectly at the topic, the way you can see something in the dim light more clearly if you don't look directly at it. I think he prefers to grasp the situation as a whole, with his eyes, his intuition, and his heart, rather than try to reduce it to simple, clumsy, crude words. I think he is like Hunter in that way, who for all his mastery of language, who could speak so clearly, elegantly, and with power through the Word, ultimately found them inadequate. It was as if to speak too plainly about a delicate topic was like looking at the sun with no eye protection. It is too bright, harsh, and unendurable. Better to filter it to see the subtle details, the fine points. Instead of asking me how I was handling the divorce, he would invite me out to Owl Farm for the weekend and just observe me, perhaps ask how Sandy was doing, not in a sneaky or deceptive way, but in a searching and exploratory way, so that I didn't even know I was being examined. I have an image of a doctor exploring an injury with long, delicate fingers, carefully searching out the contours of the wound under the skin, hardly pressing at all, more sensing, then pressing a bit here, just enough to cause a gentle reaction. All that time I thought Hunter was not paying attention, he was paying close attention.

On the other hand, what did he know about fathering? His own father had died when he was a teenager. Maybe he was just winging it, trusting his instincts, hoping for the best. Just as I am. I believe now that he was paying attention, and that he always loved me, but that's not the same thing as fathering.

That spring I had decided to go to England on a junior year abroad program through the University of Colorado the following fall. A friend of mine from boarding school had spent a semester in France and had written me many letters about her adventures there, which compelled me to create my own adventure. Susannah and I talked about it and agreed that though we loved each other and got along wonderfully, we were both very unhappy. Our comfortable life together, our comfortable and cute apartment in downtown Boulder, our comfortable routines, were not enough, not nearly enough. We each had to find something for ourselves. I thought it was in England, and Susannah thought she might find it at home in Virginia where she was born and raised.

That summer Stevens and I went on a trip to Russia, which was still a part of the Soviet Union at that time. My grandmother Leah made arrangements for us to join a tour, which was the only practical way to see the USSR. Individual travelers were discouraged. It was an odd arrangement—two twenty-year-olds from Colorado and about sixteen retired folks from central Florida. We met up with the group in New York and flew to Oslo for a night, then on to Leningrad (now Saint Petersburg). It was midsummer and Leningrad is very far north, so that the sun didn't set until eleven p.m. or so, and it didn't get dark until well after midnight, only to start getting light a few hours later. I remember that we could see a monument commemorating the Siege of Leningrad in World War II from our hotel window.

Western visitors were carefully monitored and controlled. We stayed at approved tourist hotels and had a Soviet guide with our group at all times, though Stevens and I did some exploring on our own, apparently without supervision, though we were paranoid that we were being watched or followed. In Moscow, we walked from our hotel to a market several blocks away. The market was rather small, dim, and dingy, and had a limited selection of goods, and not very many of them. The produce section was sparse. It was a remarkable contrast to American supermarkets, which are huge, brightly lit, colorful, and bursting with food.

We flew from Leningrad to Moscow, and from Moscow to the Republic of Georgia. At that time the USSR was monolithic, and I had no understanding or appreciation for the myriad cultures and nations that were collected under that vast umbrella, far broader and varied than the states within the United States. The USSR stretched from Western Europe to the Pacific Ocean and from the Arctic Circle to the Middle East—it bordered Turkey, Iran, Afghanistan, and Pakistan, and bordered the entire northern Chinese border, very nearly touching Japan. In Tbilisi, Georgia, we were offered good money for our Levi's as we walked cautiously through the ancient, narrow, curving streets of the old city, which looked like it had sprung up out of the earth, being the same color and texture. We took the Trans-Siberian Railway from Irkutsk to Khabarovsk and stopped in villages that probably looked much the same as they did five hundred years ago, with muddy dirt lanes, crooked wooden fences, and thatched houses. Merchants gathered on the train platform to sell fruit, cigarettes, and goods to the travelers for the few minutes we were in the station, and then we would pull away and disappear, and the village would fall back a few hundred years until the next train arrived a few days later. The Siberia I saw from the train consisted of vast forests, plains, and rolling hills. We traveled through it for three days and saw only a handful of villages along the railroad.

When Stevens and I returned three weeks later to the United States, it was time to pack up the apartment in preparation for England, and for Susannah to head back home to Virginia. A friend of ours offered to drive a truck full of my boxes to Woody Creek for storage at Owl Farm, and so the three of us, Steve Evans, Susannah, and myself, went to see Hunter and Maria. It was an ancient panel truck from the '40s or '50s and though it was durable and roomy, it had no heat. As we drove over 12,000-foot Independence Pass outside of Aspen, on a cool late summer day, we shivered under blankets and had to stop at a café in Leadville for an hour or two to chase the incipient frostbite from our fingers and toes.

Hunter tried to prepare me for my adventure. He lent me a red Woolrich hunting jacket and his correspondent's raincoat. I say lent, because it was rare for Hunter to give something outright. He might lend it indefinitely, but he wanted to know that he could get it back, if he really wanted it. There was a handwritten list on the back of one of the kitchen cabinet doors that listed all the items he had lent to me over the years.

Hunter was a deeply sentimental man, and like most sentimentalists, he was a pack rat, because such people, and I am one, confer on objects the essence of a person, place, or event. They are tangible reminders of the good and significant, and they are more than simply reminders, they are talismans, objects consecrated by memory. They have magical properties and they are not to be lightly disposed of or given away, because in losing them we lose a part of our memory, and memories are the bricks of the houses of our selves, our lives. That entity that we think of as our self is built on memories, of what we have done, where we have been, whom we have known and loved and fought. That house is our refuge, and also it can be our prison in which we are chained to our sins and regrets. We use our memories to define ourselves, for better or for worse. If, as the Buddhists say, fear and desire are the forces that propel us through our lives, then memories are the road behind, and the road ahead is a projection of the road behind. We expect to be who we have been.

Hunter's house was filled with memorabilia, the kitchen walls a couple of layers thick with letters, pins, photographs, newspaper clippings, notes, posters, postcards, invitations, contact sheets, awards, proclamations, memos, flags, scarves, bar coasters, buttons, and anything else that could be held up by tape or pushpin. The lower layers were usually ragged around the edges and tinted the deep yellowish brown of cigarette smoke, for they had been on the walls for twenty years or more. Every horizontal surface had things on it—statues, figures, stuffed animals, bones, knives, balls, boxes of filigreed silver or inlaid bronze, trays of ebony, an abalone shell, all things he had been given or had collected during his life at Owl Farm and in the years before that when he had traveled like a nomad around the country, becoming a writer. Owl Farm and everything in it anchored him.

Hunter was deeply rooted in Owl Farm. He had grown up in one house, on Ransdell Avenue in Louisville, Kentucky. That is where he and his two brothers were born, where he lived when his father died, where he read and wrote until he was seventeen and was thrown in jail for a month and then into the air force. From that point on, he never returned to Louisville to live. He traveled extensively from the time he was seventeen until he was about thirty, from Kentucky to Florida to the Eastern Seaboard, to California and Colorado, with visits to many other states on the way. He first lived in Woody Creek in 1963, but California pulled him back, and it wasn't until 1966 that he returned to Woody Creek. Even then, he didn't plan to stay long. He had all kinds of ideas about where he would go next. Back to California, maybe to Europe, back to South America, but it never happened. Within a few years he took root in Woody Creek; maybe it was the land, the quiet, the privacy, maybe it was the people he met, maybe it was having a family, or maybe he was just tired of moving all the time. Whatever the reasons, he took root, and for the next thirty-nine years he never left for any length of time. From that point on he had a home that he always came back to.

He wrote all of his best books there, with the exception of *Hell's Angels,* which allowed him to buy Owl Farm in the first place. He evolved from a freelance reporter to a writer to a legend while living there.

When he bought the house, he transformed it into his own creation—the War Room downstairs, where he wrote *Fear and Loathing in Las Vegas,* the living room, which was one of three hearts of the house, along with the kitchen and the bedroom. The living room was the social heart of the house for the first thirteen years or so, with the giant fireplace, the eight giant speakers surrounding the room, the books, the couch, and the Morris chair like a throne from which Hunter would hold court. There are bullet marks in the brick over the fireplace, and the andirons were made by a friend.

The War Room was the creative heart of the house up until my parents separated. It was Hunter's hideout. More than an office, it was his sanctum, with its own giant fireplace, no windows, significant books along one wall, and the typewriter. It was the place where he would not be disturbed, where he could be alone and thrash out the words, battle with his writer's block, or drift in a drug- or alcohol-induced stupor.

After 1980 or so, the kitchen became the creative and social heart. With satellite television and no wife and child to distract him, it was natural that he would take up residence there, and that friends and visitors would find him there. With football, basketball, CNN, or the Playboy Channel in the background, he wrote, talked on the phone, entertained guests, screamed, ate, threw things, read the newspaper, did his drugs, and told stories for the next twenty-five years.

Then there is the land itself. Land and space were very important to Hunter. Having privacy and space around him, where he could not be hassled or evicted, where he could sit on his porch naked, and where he could shoot large-caliber pistols from his front doorway. He was, after all, a Kentucky hillbilly, and he was ferocious in his defense of the rights of individuals to live and act as they chose, so long as it didn't cause harm to others. If he wanted to build a bonfire, dance naked, and play loud music in the middle of the night, by god he could. If he wanted to blow up propane/gasoline bombs on a winter night with a 12-gauge shotgun, he could—and did. If he wanted to tape large posters of celebrities to plywood sheets and blow large holes in them in his front yard on a Monday afternoon or a Thursday evening, he could. No one would question or try to stop him, because it was his land, his domain. As he said once in an interview, the United States was probably the only country in the world where he could live as he did. Few others would have tolerated him.

The correspondent's raincoat he lent me was part of his history, part of him, and I think that is why he could not give it to me, but only lend it. He also gave me, for that year, the rent from the tenant in the cabin next door, $550 a month, which gave me enough to buy food, clothes, books, and to travel cheaply on weekends and breaks. It was his only steady income, but it made my life much simpler, since I did not have to wonder each month if I was going to get any money, and it removed the need for desperate transatlantic phone calls in which I would have to nag him. It was generous, and it was wise, the wisdom of a man who knows himself.

I went to England at the end of September and met with my fellow students from CU. I knew nobody. I was alone again. As I had been at Concord, at Tufts, and in New York. That first night in London I was alone in my small room in the rooming house. I was amazed to feel so alone again. It was so familiar and so dreadful. The next day we took the train to Lancaster, in northwest England, and that night there was a dance at our college. I had never been a dancer and I feared the crowds and the special kind of loneliness that they bring. I remember walking in the grass behind the school that night, hidden by the dark and the trees, and feeling so lonely and forsaken that I lay on the ground and sobbed for a long time. When I had no more tears, I went back to my room. A Chinese exchange student asked if I wanted to go to the dance. I could see he was feeling lonely and awkward too, and so we went. I ended up dancing, much to my surprise, and after the dance a handful of us who had met went back to someone's room, drank tea, and talked for another hour or two. That night it all changed. I became myself, though I hardly knew it at the time.

I worked hard—the classes at Lancaster were much more difficult than classes at CU—and I explored. After classes I would walk into the countryside on the little lanes, and on weekends I would catch a train, a bus, or simply hitchhike somewhere. I spent a lot of time alone, just as I had during my year at Tufts. However, I never felt lonely that year, and I had friends. There was Rosie, and Matt, and my best friend for the next few years, a fellow CU student named Elizabeth. I joined a club that offered counseling to troubled students called Nightline. Two volunteers staffed an office every night of the week from ten p.m. until seven a.m. so that a distraught student could have someone to talk to. We would sleep on the couches, and when there was a knock on the door, we'd awake from a deep sleep, open it, put on the teapot, and listen, waiting for the caffeine to take hold. I got my hair cut short so that it stood up straight. Most of the year I wore my red Woolrich coat with a keffiyeh and aviator glasses that darkened in the sunlight and turned clear indoors. I was a vegetarian and went to Gaysoc meetings with Elizabeth, who was sounding out her sexuality. I wrote letters to Susannah in my journal and then photocopied it and sent the copies to her, most everything, anyway. There were some adventures in dating that I didn't share, though we had not made any kind of agreement when we parted.

I didn't talk to Hunter much that year. He was still with Maria and trying to write *The Silk Road,* spending a fair amount of time in the Florida Keys. However, he did send me a letter once, along with a couple of postcards from a fan. He didn't read much fan mail—most of it went into a box unopened—but this was a postcard, quick to read and intriguing to Hunter. The author, Lois, was from Liverpool, an hour or two south of Lancaster, and he suggested I look her up. She was a great admirer of Hunter's and an aspiring writer herself. We exchanged letters and made plans to meet in Liverpool.

Lois read prolifically, and wrote an endless number of long, funny, thoughtful letters to her friends. I remember that she wore black most of the time, and she loved cemeteries, Samuel Beckett, The Smiths, and of course Hunter's writing, among many other things. She had been to university, but then rather than join the ranks of the wage slaves, she lived on the dole with other like-minded friends, using it as a subsistence-level artists' subsidy. Three or four people lived in one small, ratty, third-floor walkup. They ate out of cans and bought nothing new. No one had a car. She saved her money so she could travel to Wales, which she loved deeply. She would go there for a week a few times a year and walk among the hills and small towns. Lois was planning to write a novel. Her roommates were artists also. They were dirt-poor and seemed on the whole to be quite content. She invited me one weekend to join her on a trip to Wales, but for reasons I still can't explain I missed the train to Liverpool. That is one of the lingering regrets of my life. Something important was there for me, but I have no idea what it might have been. I visited her a second time in Liverpool, and we corresponded frequently and amply over the next two years. The last I heard she had given up her vow of poverty and become a mail delivery woman, which suited her schedule and proclivities well. She was one of the sanest people I have ever met.

At Lancaster the school year was arranged into three segments, with a month vacation after the first two. That first vacation I decided to visit Ralph Steadman in Maidstone, Kent, southeast of London. Ralph had been "Uncle Ralph" as long as I could remember. I still remember that summer he and Anna, his wife, came to visit us at Owl Farm and he tried to crush my head with a large rock down by the river. I explored parts of southwest England first, and then headed to Ralph's for Christmas. His home was more like a manor house, with a vast stone façade and a circular driveway of gravel set in a large green lawn bordered by oak trees. I was fortunate enough to stay in the Leonardo room, named because of the *Last Supper* mural Ralph had painted on the wall above the bed. The room was huge, at least forty feet square, with several tall windows and a set of French doors that looked out over the lawn and the creek. The ceilings were very high, fifteen feet at least. It was a room fit for a king, and it was mine for ten days. I remember sitting in that room one day at the typewriter I had set up near the French doors, working on an essay for school, and thinking that life couldn't get better than this.

When I wasn't working on a paper for school or spending time with Uncle Ralph, I borrowed his trumpet and tried to teach myself to play "Smoke Gets in Your Eyes." There was a little gazebo in his backyard with many windows and an old printing press in the center, and I would take the trumpet there and practice. At the end of my stay, he said he would give me twenty pounds toward a trumpet if I would promise to practice. I agreed, and on my way back to school I found a secondhand music store in London, and bought an old trumpet. Back at school I would practice in a classroom at night, and though I was a raw beginner, the reverb created by the sound bouncing off the tile floors and the concrete walls made it sound lovely. One night the janitor stopped by and said, "I've never heard Dvořák's *New World* Symphony so badly butchered," and then picked up the trumpet and proceeded to show me how it ought to be played.

It was a magical year. I suddenly became someone different. In some respects it was much like Tufts in the amount of time I spent alone, and yet it was completely different. I was different. I had Elizabeth and Matt and Rosie—who liked me just as I was. I bought new clothes and went to the school dances whenever I could. I was not afraid.

When I came back to the States the following summer I stopped in New York to see Laila, Hunter's ex-girlfriend. She told me that she had been going to Al-Anon and that it had been very helpful in dealing with Hunter. She invited me to a meeting and I went along. I remember the Twelve Steps were printed on a poster hanging on the wall, and I read each one and checked them off. "Okay, that's easy. Done and simple enough," all the way through the twelve points. We talked about it afterward and I think I dismissed it as something marginally interesting.

It was sometime in my senior year that I decided to look into it further. I hadn't thought of Hunter as an alcoholic before. Drinking was a part of Hunter, like his shorts, his Chuck Taylors, the TarGard cigarette holder, his unpredictable anger, and his bow-legged walk. He was just Hunter, and it had never occurred to me that he could be any different than he was, or that there could be an explanation for his behavior. However, for all the progress we had made over the past eight or nine years, our relationship was still filled with tension and I was exceedingly wary of him. Though I didn't hate him any longer, I was still angry with him for being so difficult, unpredictable, volatile, unreasonable, and selfish. He was often such a bastard.

My relationship with Hunter was not like my far more conventional relationship with my son, a long and steady path made up of thousands of daily events over the years, none a big deal by itself, but notable for the strength of the foundation they make up. Instead, it was made up of relatively few but very intense events, each of which built up or tore down the foundation so that the change was clear. One of these events was my decision to go through the Twelve-Step process, for real this time.

What exactly compelled me to seek out a Twelve-Step meeting in Boulder, I do not remember. However, I was not happy. For all my friendships, adventure, and discovery during my year in England, I was still not happy. I went to a meeting of Adult Children of Alcoholics, a subgroup of Al-Anon that focused on adult children specifically, rather than Al-Anon's more general mission of serving friends, spouses, and family members of an alcoholic. The Twelve-Step programs were popular in Boulder then and there were plenty of meetings to choose from.

One of the most effective aspects of the meeting format is, first, the chance to listen to other people talk about their lives without any obligation to reply to them or to advise them, and second, the opportunity to talk without being advised or replied to. I listened and heard familiar stories. The more I listened, the more I began to understand that my unhappiness was not unique. I began attending meetings regularly and got a sponsor, which is the first step toward working through the Twelve Steps.

Hearing these stories helped me to understand that I was far from alone in my suffering. There were a lot of people like me, some worse off, some better off, but all of them suffering to some degree.

Over that first year I came to the understanding that Hunter's suffering was not unique either, and that at least a part of it was the result of his drinking. And therefore a part of my suffering was the result of his drinking. During one of my visits to Owl Farm I decided to write him a letter. I did not trust myself to be able to speak what I wanted to tell him, nor did I trust Hunter to listen. So I wrote a him a letter.

I don't have that letter now, but I remember it was an accusation and a declaration: an accusation that he was indeed an alcoholic, and a declaration that I wasn't going to assist him with his drinking. I told him I wasn't going to get him drinks anymore. Furthermore, if he didn't watch his temper with me I would leave. It was a page or two, typed. I gave it to him in an envelope and went into the living room where I waited for him to read it.

He didn't take it well. He gave it back, marked up. He had circled words or sentences in red pen, and written words like "Balls!," "Chickenshit!," and "Evil Poppa" in the margins or across the page, in response to things I had written. I had been warned not to expect hugs and kisses, but his reaction was still a deep disappointment to me. We didn't talk about it, and we avoided each other for the rest of the day. However, the next time he wanted a beer or ice for his whiskey, he didn't ask me. He got it himself or asked Deborah to get it for him.

On a roll now, I gave a similar letter to my mother that year. I don't have that letter either, and though it was no doubt accusatory and needlessly harsh, she took it much better than Hunter did, and over years and decades we have talked, struggled, adjusted, compromised, and fought toward a very different but just as necessary reconciliation.

That year I realized a couple of fundamental truths: whatever my father's greater virtues were as a writer, a warrior, and a wise man, in his daily life he was a basket case, or in the vocabulary of the time, dysfunctional. He was unpredictable, unreliable, unreasonable, and given to sudden fits of rage, and if I was confused and disturbed when I went into his world, it was no surprise—it was a confusing and disturbing world he had created around him. The second fundamental truth is that I did not have to be part of his craziness. I could simply leave if it got too weird, just walk out the door, or even drive home.

To many people these truths may seem obvious and self-evident, as if I stated that, at the age of twenty-three, I realized that the sun always rises in the east, and that a hot stove burns. But to me it was new. It meant that I was no longer at the mercy of his madness. It is hard to describe the sense of freedom it gave me to know that now I stood outside of Hunter's world, and that I could step in and out of it at will. I had been like some animal that had lived in a cage so long that even after the cage was removed, the animal still acted as if the bars of the cage were there, and didn't bother to check, because they had always been there. And then I looked up and saw that they were gone.

I spent another six years in the Twelve-Step program in Boulder. There was a particularly rigorous approach in Boulder in those days which took the Twelve-Step process and added a bit of est (Erhard Seminars Training) and a pinch of existential philosophy. This approach required an exhaustive inventory of every incident I could remember, an analysis of those incidents to determine a core set of beliefs, a re-examination of each incident to see how I used it to reinforce those core beliefs, and then a final review of all the incidents to see if there were other, more accurate interpretations. The whole process took a few years. For instance, I may have a memory of my mother yelling at me when I was a child because I spilled a pot on the stove. At the time it served as more proof that there was something wrong with me. Upon objective review, I realize that my mother was yelling at me because she was afraid I was going to get hurt, that it's a normal thing for children to spill things, and that it has no bearing or relation to my essential competence or value as a person. In other words, it highlighted how I had interpreted events and memories to suit my existing convictions, rather than be open to changing those convictions based on the facts. If my mind is like a courtroom, then I act more like a courtroom lawyer who selects and arranges facts to support my predetermined guilt or innocence, rather than like the impartial jury coming to a conclusion based on the facts. In theory, once I understand this, I can readjust my interpretations of people and events not only in the past but in the present. As a result, my thoughts, feelings, and actions are now in accord with reality.

This program was not the Answer, the Cure, the Fix I was looking for, but through it, and with the help of my fellow Program travelers, I began to understand that there might be more than one way to interpret my experiences. This was a revelation which I spent the next six years exploring.

In England I had taken mostly literature classes, Victorian and modern literature, and had found that I loved English literature. Upon my return to Boulder for the first of my two senior years, I declared English literature my major. I have never regretted that decision. I loved English literature because it was full of meaning, it addressed the difficulties, paradoxes, conundrums, and puzzles of life through stories, rather than indirectly through business, economics, psychology, or the sciences. Literature is essentially composed of stories, and I love stories, especially complicated ones. By complicated I don't mean twisting and turning plots like a thriller or a mystery, but complicated in the sense of ambiguous and subtle, where right and wrong are not so easily determined, where individual will does not always overcome circumstance or external forces, where good as we understand it does not always prevail.

I loved literature because it helped me to understand my world, and as a literature major I got to read really good books every day, discuss what I had read, and write about it. Hunter had said that the only value of going to college is that it gives a

On the front steps of my apartment
in Boulder, Colorado, 1988

person four years to read. Hunter was probably satisfied with my choice of a major.

I graduated summa cum laude with a degree in literature in 1988. Hunter made it to the graduation ceremony this time, along with Sandy, Deb, and Maria. I don't know what it took to get him there, but I was very grateful and am still.

SEVEN

Getting Straight: ages 24 to 30

The ashram—Jennifer—The burning of the ham—The
Bomb—The wedding—"I never liked you anyway."

HST TIMELINE

1988   *Generation of Swine* (compilation of *San Francisco Examiner*
       columns) published.
1989   Hunter awarded New York Library's "Literary Lion" award.
1990   "99 Days" trial (Gail Palmer-Slater accuses Hunter of attacking
       her).
       Songs of the Doomed published.
1991   Hunter covers the Roxanne and Peter Pulitzer trial in Palm
       Beach.
       Proposes and gets a book contract for *Polo Is My Life.*
1992   Clinton runs for president, Hunter an unofficial advisor to the
       campaign.
1994   *Better Than Sex* published.

DURING COLLEGE I had a part-time job at a local desk-
top publishing company. When I graduated, I started
working full-time there, and started doing technical art on the
computer for math textbooks. In 1990, I had decided to spend a
few months at a yoga ashram in Massachusetts.

The ashram was called Kripalu Center for Yoga and Health, in Lenox, Massachusetts, in the heart of the Berkshires. It offered a number of programs, from a day to a couple of months, in different aspects of yoga. It was moderately expensive, and catered, for the most part, to reasonably well-off New Englanders. However, it was also an ashram, though this was somewhat hidden from the regular guests. It had been started and was run by a fellow named Amrit Desai, who was the spiritual leader, and was staffed by residents. Some had been with Gurudev, as he was known to his devotees, for many years, while others stayed for a year or so. Like a monastery, there was a Rule that all the residents lived under, which included a vow of celibacy for all unmarried residents. They had an internship program, in which a person could live at the ashram for three or four months at no cost in return for full-time labor. Interns lived the life of an ashram resident, getting up at five a.m. for morning yoga, working at their assigned tasks during the day, attending evening devotional services, and taking part in the religious celebrations. I signed up for the internship and arrived in the summer. I was assigned to the kitchen crew, where my job was to wash dishes, serve meals, clean, and do other duties as assigned.

I enthusiastically committed myself to the lifestyle, aided by the knowledge that it was only for four months. I practiced yoga every morning, half asleep, I sang at satsang and chanted Om with three hundred other people. I chewed each bite of my food three hundred times before swallowing, bowed to Gurudev, followed the Rule, and was in general a most devoted and willing novitiate.

The internship was called Spiritual Lifestyle Training, or SLT, and SLT interns were encouraged to dedicate themselves fully to the lifestyle for the duration of their stay. We were discouraged from spending much time off the grounds, and the schedule, which consisted of working seven days a week with two half days off, made it impossible to go for more than a few hours. On my half days I would ride my bicycle along the rolling and winding roads of the Berkshires, through tiny towns, have a snack of ice cream or pancakes, and then ride back to the center. The countryside was stunning, not unlike England. It was very lush, with many, many trees, small lakes and ponds, lovely old farmhouses, barns, and churches, tiny cemeteries from the 1800s on narrow back roads, and enough sun to keep away the gloom, yet not so much that I didn't appreciate it deeply when it came out bright and clear. My work crew was headed by a very sincere, gentle, and quiet young man named Anup, who was among the tiny group who had taken a lifelong vow of obedience and celibacy, just as Catholic monks and nuns, after a trial period, commit themselves to the life of obedience and chastity. He had given away all his possessions when he came to Kripalu, and his room consisted of little more than a small altar to Gurudev, a few simple clothes, and a few photos. He didn't even have a mattress, but preferred to sleep on the carpeted floor with a thin blanket. He was one of the calmest, most sincere, and most peaceful people I have ever met. He was technically my manager, though that word completely misrepresents the situation.

Anup treated work as a spiritual path, and the members of his crew as novices to be mentored, and this made all the difference. Anup encouraged us to look at our jobs as service rather than drudgery, and to use it as an opportunity to practice acceptance, and to find through acceptance, grace. If Anup had not believed it himself, this would have been inexcusable bullshit to feed us, but he was completely sincere, and his sincerity dispelled my cynicism and doubts. It was hard work—at lunch I would head straight for my bunk in the dormitory and instantly fall asleep for a half hour—but I never resented it, never felt that it was below me, that as a smart, college-educated, and by god, honors graduate, I should be doing some work more meaningful and challenging. I attribute this to Anup's sincerity and to his example, and to the power of a group committed to a common goal and view of reality.

All of us interns took his challenge, though he didn't present it as one. Each morning we would crowd into Anup's tiny office next to the kitchen and talk about the practicalities of the day and who was assigned to what job, and then Anup would give us a lesson, usually a reading or a reflection. We would meditate for a few minutes, and then join in a quiet communal Om, before heading off to crank up the dishwashing machine, a giant industrial dishwasher, dryer, and conveyer belt that took up a significant chunk of the commercial kitchen and required six or eight people to run it. It was named "Brother Lawrence," after the monk who found grace while washing dishes at his monastery.

One day I was on my lunch break, sitting outside on the kitchen loading dock. Perhaps I had talked to Hunter recently, perhaps I was reflecting on something he had done or said that angered me, when it struck me, and it did strike me like a thing from outside, that the only way that I would have any peace with my father, the only way I would have any kind of satisfying relationship, was if I made an effort to move toward him, rather than wait for him to stop or at least moderate his craziness with me. At the same time I understood that this meant accepting, on a deep and real level, that he was not going to change. He would not stop drinking every day, he would not stop snorting cocaine, he would not restrain himself from going into rages, demanding to be the center of attention, and having unrealistic expectations of those around him. He would not call me more often, or write me more letters, or tell me he loved me. What he had been, what he was, he would continue to be. If I wanted to be closer to him, I had to move. This concept of acceptance was very familiar to me from the Twelve-Step program, and I had been thinking and writing in my journal about Hunter quite a lot at Kripalu. This day, though, the insight took root in my heart rather than my head. I sat on the loading dock reflecting on this wisdom, surprised by the suddenness of the insight.

I'd like to say that this insight changed my life, but that is not true, nor did it result in a sudden breakthrough with Hunter. However, it never left me, even when I returned to Colorado and resumed my normal life. It was a background awareness, the conscious realization that I wanted and needed to be closer to my father, and that it was up to me to move toward him. Consistent with our communication style up until then, I didn't tell him about my sudden insight, nor did I ever say much about Kripalu to him, and he didn't ask.

When I completed my four months at Kripalu I was ambivalent about leaving because it had been such a powerful and intense experience that I wanted to prolong. I agonized over my decision, whether to stay on or return, and finally chose to return to Boulder. Several years later I felt better about my decision when I learned that Gurudev confessed to sleeping with several of his senior female disciples over many years, causing a major crisis, which eventually led to his resignation in disgrace and the disbanding of the ashram. Kripalu became a purely secular health and wellness center, which it remains today. I never told Hunter about this, but I'm sure this would not have surprised him one bit, but rather than condemning Gurudev, he probably would have wondered why the ashram community was so shocked and disillusioned.

Once I graduated from college, I no longer received any money from Hunter, and this was good. It meant that I no longer had to endure the madness of trying to get something from him, particularly money. No more nervous phone calls, no more fear and panic. It is no way to live, being dependent on someone else for money, especially being at the mercy of an admittedly irresponsible and unreliable man. Meanwhile, I was still slogging through the Twelve-Step process and establishing a beachhead of sanity. The more I looked at my life with my parents, the more I realized how strange, confusing, and peculiar it was. Now I had a normal life in Boulder, I worked at a regular job, I paid my bills, I did not have to deal with the excitement and self-inflicted crises that Hunter lived in constantly.

IT WAS A YEAR OR SO after my return from Kripalu that I started dating Jennifer. She, her partner, and my live-in girlfriend at the time, Cyndi, and I had been friends for a couple of years, double-dating frequently. Jennifer and I would sit across from each other at the restaurant and talk about family dynamics, dysfunction, and personal and spiritual growth, while our dates talked about who knows what. After this had happened several times, Cyndi suggested that Jen and I sit diagonally from each other to discourage us from talking so intently to the exclusion of our dates. Maybe she knew something that we didn't, because it came as a surprise to us when, a few months after we had each broken up with our partners for reasons completely unrelated to our friendship, Jennifer and I found ourselves becoming aware of an urge to be more than simply friends.

Jennifer came from a similarly unusual background. Her father, Bill, had abandoned a job as a successful salesman for Texaco in order to be his own boss as the owner of a gas station in Brighton, Colorado, just outside Denver. Unfortunately that coincided with the OPEC oil crisis in the '70s, and the family suffered financial catastrophe including the loss of their house, business, and most of their possessions. The stress caused her father to be hospitalized for a serious ulcer that nearly killed him. Kay, her mother, left her father and took Jennifer's two sisters to Iowa. Jennifer stayed with her father for a while, and then joined her mother and sisters, later attending the University of Iowa. Eventually Bill followed, getting a job repairing the giant injection-molding machines at a toothbrush factory and starting his own hand-built furniture business on the side.

Like Susannah, Jennifer was smart, funny, artsy, and beautiful, but unlike Susannah, I wasn't her student. We first connected while talking about our crazy childhoods and unconventional fathers. She too knew what it was like to while away the time in a bar while her parents drank, and she knew what it was like to grow up with a father with keen insight, disregard for convention, and a painfully sharp tongue. We both loved books and poetry, which she wrote, and we both had been lonely outsiders. And she was just odd and up for adventures, which I loved. One weekend we took turns blindfolding each other and leading the other around Boulder. Another weekend we spent all day gathering small branches and twigs to create a mobile made with the branches, black thread, superglue, and old TV tubes. We both liked old electronics, not because they were useful, but because they were beautiful. At a junk store we found a portable EKG machine from the '50s in a sturdy blond wooden case, and celebrated such a lucky find.

We also had drugs in common. Not that we did drugs together, but we both had done plenty of experimentation when younger, and had each chosen to stop at a certain point (though I had just about given up my experimentation phase by the time she got started in college). It was wonderful to be able to talk about the benefits and downsides of drugs and drinking without feeling freakish, and also to be with someone who didn't feel the need to keep doing them.

The spiritual connection was very important also. We both were seeking peace and clarity through spirituality and personal growth. We could easily talk about what we had learned working with therapists, about yoga and gurus and meditation. After we had been together about a year, I learned about a ten-day Buddhist meditation retreat, which required not only silence but forbade eye contact with the other participants for the entire ten days, including mealtimes. I asked her if she wanted to go. She said of course.

I wanted to introduce her to Hunter. I spent that Christmas at Owl Farm, and Jennifer came up for New Year's. She had been a fan of his writing for years before we had met, ever since she had been active in political campaigning first as a canvass director and later as a campaign manager for a national grassroots political organization that advocated a freeze in nuclear armament. She had read many of his books and was especially fond of *Fear and Loathing on the Campaign Trail '72*, also my favorite.

From the time we started dating seriously, marriage had been lurking in the background, though neither of us was anxious to ever get married, given our parents' poor track record in that area. At one point I was working as a computer consultant for the company where she worked, and we were sitting outside on the stairs. I said, "I have this crazy fear that we're going to get married." Jennifer laughed and said, "That's a crazy idea. Don't worry about it. We're just dating." A year later we were living together, and the next year we were engaged.

The weekend of the engagement Jen and I stayed at a ranch in Utah for a few days. Though it was a working ranch, it was actually more of a private park owned by an old East Coast family. The ranch was on a high mesa just across the Colorado-Utah border, on the edge of Colorado National Monument, noted for its spectacular, deep canyons and sandstone mesas. The night before we left, I had been watching Jennifer sleep, and I wondered what I would do if something happened to her. I didn't want to lose her. I didn't want to lose this. I loved her very much and I wanted to go deeper with her.

On the way home from the ranch, just before we hit the paved road on the mesa, I asked Jennifer to marry me, and she agreed. We hadn't planned on seeing Hunter that weekend, but Aspen was on the way from Grand Junction to Denver, so we decided to make our announcement in person. This was before cell phones, so we stopped along the way and called Owl Farm. Deborah answered and said he was in Basalt at Chefy's, one of his restaurant hideaways. We found him sitting with Nicole and a couple of other people we didn't know. It didn't seem right to tell him in front of strangers, so we ended up returning to Owl Farm with him and Nicole. When we got to the house, though, a game was on and a few friends had come out to watch. Finally I said, "Hunter, I have something to tell you." I took him aside and I told him we had decided to get married.

He was ecstatic. He whooped, he smiled, he demanded cham-

*With Hunter and Jennifer at Owl Farm, 1994. Hunter is
wearing his hat of unborn wolf pup fur, or so he claimed.*

pagne for a toast, he went searching for gifts to give us, finally
settling on a mounted rattlesnake's head under glass. He put on
Celtic music—the Chieftains—and demanded that Deborah
and Nicole get cameras to capture this moment. Deb had been
the unofficial photographer for Owl Farm for years, and Nicole
was in charge of video.

He started talking about the wedding, how it had to be a good-
size wedding, but not too big, how it would be the event of the
year that everyone would want to be invited to, but there would
only be room for a select group. Gerry Goldstein, a high-profile
criminal defense lawyer, and Dan Dibble, a longtime Aspenite,
got into the groove, discussing how people would compete for
invitations by sending the biggest, grandest engagement presents. We talked for a long time, half-seriously planning, joking, and laughing. It was one of those magic moments with my

father when everything was right. Finally, it was time for us to go. We both had to be at work the next day and we still had a three-and-a-half-hour drive ahead of us. Hunter insisted we have a ceremony before leaving. He told Deb to bring out the sugar-cured ham from the back refrigerator, probably left over from the previous Christmas. Deb protested that it was no longer edible, but Hunter had other ideas. He set the ham in a broiler pan and put it on a side table in the kitchen. He said that the burning of the ham was an old Kentucky tradition to celebrate an engage-

Hunter and Deb at our engagement party, 1993

ment. We had to set the ham on fire. He took a bottle of fine scotch from the top of the refrigerator, which served as the liquor cabinet, poured it liberally over the ham, and held a flame to it. Nothing. He tried a higher proof, maybe a Wild Turkey 101. Still nothing. He tried a variety of liquors, none of which worked, until he dug out a bottle of Everclear from behind all the other bottles, which gave a bright, clean-burning flame to the ham and fulfilled the requirements of that old Kentucky tradition. A few days later we received one more engagement gift in the mail: a bouquet of plastic lilies with a tiny Christmas bulb in the middle of each flower. Out from among the stems came a thin green cord with a plug on the end.

A few months later there was an engagement party for us at the Basalt house of Carol and Palmer Hood, who years before had given me a place to hide, and for whom I had assassinated gophers. Hunter had taken an interest in the engagement party guest list. We had our friends we wanted to invite, and Hunter had his friends. I'm sure Hunter initially hoped to host the party at a club in Aspen, maybe the Snowmass Club, which was his preferred restaurant around that time, but he couldn't afford it. He was going through one of his lean periods.

Hunter and money. The premise is very simple: when he had it he squandered it with such abandon and pleasure that it never lasted long, and when it ran out he borrowed until he could cobble together the next deal. The lean times lasted longer than the fat times, sometimes as long as a couple of years. The early to mid-1990s was one of those times, even though *Better Than Sex* was published in 1994. But when he had money he was usually very generous. One weekend we came to Owl Farm and found that a new set of knives had replaced the old, superior set. It turned out that the son of a friend of his had a job selling knife sets and was passing through Aspen. Hunter bought a set to help him out. One Christmas he bought handfuls of small gold ingots and gave them as presents. Hunter knew my interest in and fondness for computers, and for a wedding present he gave us a new Macintosh laptop. But in the lean times Deborah counted the pennies, kept the various creditors at bay with payments just large enough to keep them believing that they would get paid in full eventually. He would sometimes hide checks or payments from Deborah if he happened to go through the mail before she did, so he could have some spending money, damn the consequences.

The engagement party was one of the lean times, but if that bothered Hunter, it didn't bother us. Hunter talked with Jen's parents, Bill and Kay, introduced them to his friends, sat for a long time at a table with our friends, none of whom he knew, and flirted with some of the young women we had invited. When the party was over, he asked Jen and me to come back to Owl Farm with a few other people. I asked him if I could invite a few of my friends. He said, "How many?" I said maybe fifteen. He hesitated, always loath to have strangers in his house or even on his property, but he agreed. He said, "We'll have to have a bomb, though." Once at the house, people wandered freely between the living room and the kitchen, although I know it made him very uncomfortable, for he asked, "Can I trust these people?" and warned me to keep an eye on them. He kept himself from saying anything hostile or rude, though he did flip on the Playboy Channel once or twice for a few minutes, just to see how people would react, especially the women.

As it was getting dark, he called for the Bomb. Years ago he had come up with a combination of bomb ingredients that yielded a spectacular fireball. It started with a coffee can full of gasoline. Either taped to or right in front of the can he would set a small propane canister, the kind you use for a camping stove. Finally, he would stick several square exploding targets, two-inch Styrofoam squares with explosives embedded in them, to the propane canister. The device was triggered by a load of double-0 buckshot from a 12-gauge shotgun. The ball-bearing-size shot would set off the exploding target, puncture the propane canister, and punch the gasoline can so that it would spray up into the air. The exploding target would ignite the propane, which would in turn ignite the gasoline. The tricky part was hitting the target dead-on. One or two pellets wouldn't do it. It required a bull's-eye.

Hunter asked Deb to put together the bomb, and then he placed it on a stump in the side yard. He was a natural showman and had used the bomb preparation time to get my friends excited to see the show, many of whom had never shot a gun, much less set off a propane-gasoline bomb in their yards.

He told me that I would have to set off the bomb. I had always been a good shot, but there was a lot of pressure. Everyone had crowded behind me, and Hunter stood beside me. Hunter's friends had seen this before, so a missed shot would not be nearly as disappointing to them as it would be to our friends, especially after all the buildup. I was most concerned about Hunter's reaction if I missed. I didn't want to disappoint him. I wanted to prove myself and provide a good spectacle, but more important was proving to Hunter that I could do this thing.

Perhaps I wanted to prove an element of my manhood to him. Hunter was a man's man and had been from his childhood. He was large, strong, and dominant. He smoked cigarettes and drank, drove fast, and attracted beautiful women. He rode motorcycles and took risks. He knew how to fight and how to intimidate people verbally to avoid a fight. On the other hand, I didn't date until I was a senior in high school, never smoked, had never been in a fight, and drank very rarely. I loved books, computers, and fantasy role-playing games like Dungeons and Dragons. I didn't care much for sports and preferred acting in plays. My friends were like me—awkward, smart, not cute, and frequently lonely. I was a nerd.

So that night, holding the 12-gauge shotgun to my shoulder, I wanted to show my father that I was skilled in at least one of the arts that he valued, that somehow that would establish my credentials as a man, if not a man's man. I took aim, took my time, and pulled the trigger. There was an explosion, the gun slammed back into my shoulder, and a giant yellow fireball rose into the sky, lasting a second or so. When it was over, everyone cheered and Hunter slapped me on the shoulder and congratulated me on fine shooting. I was happy, I felt that I had staked out a small claim on the turf of manhood, and I was glad I had made my father proud.

Jennifer and I got married in August of 1994. Throughout the planning process, Hunter wanted to make sure that we had the right kind of wedding. He didn't want it to be cheap— a grange hall or Knights of Columbus event room was out of the question. He was relieved to find out that we were having the wedding not in a church, but at a log cabin restaurant in an old mining town called Gold Hill in the foothills outside of Boulder. As with the engagement party, he wanted to be involved with the invitation list. We would fax our list to him and he would review it and make notes and suggestions. He was glad to know we were inviting his brother Davison and his family, as well as my family on my mother's side. We told him we were inviting my preschool teacher and one of my teachers from the Aspen Community School. He was glad that we had respect for past attachments and the Aspen community that I was a part of, though I hadn't lived there for a long time and when I did visit I hardly ever left Owl Farm.

He sent out several requests to people such as Jimmy Buffett, Jann Wenner, Ralph Steadman, Ed Bradley, and Don Johnson, as well as a number of other friends of his. When I think now of why he wanted us to invite them, I think it was a combination of "doing the right thing" and consciously reinforcing the bonds among his community by inviting them to be part of a very important ceremony. When I attended my cousins' weddings, which were large, traditional affairs, the parents' friends were invited. It is so ironic that as a father Hunter passed on so few traditions, yet he possessed these traditional reflexes that would show themselves so unexpectedly.

Hunter and Ed Bradley in the kitchen at Owl Farm. Ed was one of Hunter's closest friends and a man he respected deeply.

He was also wondering what to wear, and had suggestions for me. He insisted that I wear a tuxedo, but not just any tuxedo, it had to be an Armani. We explained that I couldn't rent an Armani tux, at least not in Denver, at least not in our price range. He was disappointed, but he understood. If he had had the money, I think he would have ordered one from New York, or just bought one for me, crazy as that would have been, but that was not an option, and I didn't care.

He met Sandy's father for the first time at our wedding. George Taylor Conklin III was a very traditional, thoughtful, conservative man who started working for the Guardian Life Insurance Company in 1939 and retired as chairman of the board in the 1980s. He was a quiet, brilliant man who was in many ways Hunter's polar opposite: a Republican, an economist, and an academic who had graduated from Dartmouth and gotten his PhD in economics from NYU while working at Guardian. I've only heard parts of the story, and perhaps someday my mother will tell more of it, but the gist is that she and her father had very different ideas about how Sandy should proceed in life, and he didn't like the sound of this Thompson fellow, who seemed to represent the destruction of everything her father believed in and that had made him successful. When Sandy and Hunter eventually got married, it was without his consent. More than thirty years later he finally met Hunter at the marriage of his grandson. Later he said he was impressed by him and that he seemed to be a real gentleman.

We had decided to pay for the wedding ourselves. Though it was very inexpensive by most standards, about $10,000 including our honeymoon and vacation time, none of our parents were in a financial position to give us substantial help. Hunter didn't mention it, but I think it was difficult for him not to be able to help us. We did ask Hunter to pay for the rehearsal dinner at the Med restaurant in Boulder, which he agreed to, though he never showed up.

Oliver Treibick lived up at the end of the road in the old lumber town of Lenado. He was Hunter's closest friend, his confidant, and his advisor. Oliver was another big man, well over six feet. He had a little goatee and smoked cigars, so that he looked like an aging biker, and in fact he owned a couple of Harleys that he would ride in good weather. I don't know just what Oliver's job was; he said it had something to do with building cell phone towers. He would fly to New York City and work there for a few weeks, then come back for a week or so. Whatever he was doing was paying him well, and one day he heard from Hunter that we were having some trouble raising enough money for the wedding. He called and told me to send him the wedding budget. He said, I'm in a position to help you, and your dad isn't right now. So send me the budget, and don't you dare tell him that I'm doing this. Oliver ended up giving us $1,000 toward the wedding expenses and also paid for Jennifer's wedding dress. Hunter never knew.

Hunter did pay for one other thing. A week or so before the wedding, Deb came down to Boulder to help us with the final planning and preparation. When she learned that the ceremony was going to take place outside in the yard next to the restaurant in the middle of the day, she told us we needed a tent. Yes, that would be nice, we said, but a tent costs several hundred dollars and we can't do it. She said Hunter couldn't sit out in the sun for two hours in the middle of the day. She called Hunter and explained the situation. Later that day she informed us that there would be a tent, that she had ordered it and that Hunter was

*Hunter, Deb Fuller, me, and Jen on the front porch swing
at the Gold Hill Inn outside of Boulder, Colorado, on our
wedding day, 1994. The four of us were a family.*

going to take care of the cost. He was right, of course. It was a
longish ceremony, roughly two hours, and though we were in the
mountains and the air temperature was mild, somewhere in the
mid-70s, in Colorado's thin air the sun's rays are not buffered and
they burn and scorch.

The ceremony was to begin at eleven a.m. I was very worried
that Hunter would not make it in time. It was close to a five-hour
drive from Woody Creek, but eleven o'clock came and there he
was, with the Red Shark, the 1972 red Chrysler convertible with
the white vinyl seats. It was to be our limo after the reception.

He was very happy. His son was getting married to a good
woman. He told Jennifer several times how beautiful she looked,
and hugged us both, at one point muttering, "We'll get through

this." He was dressed in a white tuxedo with a bow tie but still wearing his Converse All-Stars. He looked elegant, distinguished, and just a bit strange.

He was a gentleman throughout the day. Sandy had asked Hunter to walk her down the aisle to their front row seats. He was not happy about this, and he asked me, "Is this important to you?" I said, "It's important to Sandy." They walked arm in arm, smiling, for the first time in around sixteen years, since their separation in 1978. At one point in the ceremony we were to light a candle, but there was a light breeze that made this difficult. Hunter joined us, pulled out his lighter, and cupped his hands around the wick as he got it to catch fire. It was a simple, thoughtful act, without drama. At one point in the ceremony we asked our parents to come up and join us for some private words. We huddled together and Hunter had his arms around Jennifer

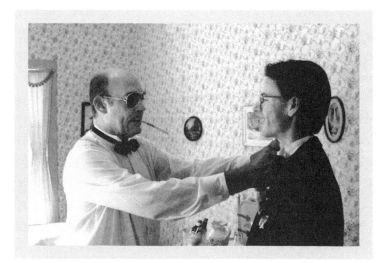

With Hunter on our wedding day. He wore a tuxedo for us, but he also wore his Chuck Taylor All-Stars.

and me. He pulled Jennifer close and said, "I never liked you anyway," and gave her a squeeze. This was his way of saying he loved her.

We had worked hard on the ceremony to make it as meaningful as we could, and though some people considered it overly long and others probably found the combination of Catholic, Hindu, and Buddhist elements unsettling at best, everyone agreed that it was a great success. The reception afterward in the restaurant was loud and festive, and Hunter was proud and happy. For months afterward he told us that everyone was talking about the wedding and how many people had said it was the best wedding they had ever been to.

I think he was happy; first of all, because I was marrying a good woman, and he wanted me to be happy. But there was more to it. Hunter was a romantic at heart, and he believed in marriage not in the contemporary practical sense of a long-term partnership defined by the spirit of compromise, acceptance, and commitment, but as a romantic adventure. He wanted me to have that adventure, and to be successful where he and Sandy had failed. Finally, I think marriage was a demonstration that I had sufficient emotional health to gain the love and confidence of a good woman like Jennifer, and that this was to some degree a pardon for his shortcomings as a father.

EIGHT

RECONCILIATION: AGES 30 TO 41

The hidden language—Better Than Sex—*The letters books—
Still cleaning the guns—Building the fire—"Ace" and the birth of
a grandson—Celebrated in Louisville——The titanium spine*

HST TIMELINE

1994   *Gonzo Papers, Vol. 4: Better Than Sex: Confessions of a Political
        Junkie* published.
1996   Hunter S. Thompson tribute in Louisville, Kentucky.
1997   *The Proud Highway* (first collection of HST letters) published.
1998   *The Rum Diary* published.
        Fear and Loathing in Las Vegas movie released.
1999   *Hell's Angels* and *Fear and Loathing in Las Vegas* released as
        Modern Library editions.
2000   *Screwjack* published.
        *Fear and Loathing in America: The Brutal Odyssey of an Outlaw
        Journalist, 1968–1976* published (second letters book).
2003   *Kingdom of Fear: Loathsome Secrets of a Star-Crossed Child in
        the Final Days of the American Century* published (collection of
        previous writings and columns).
2005   *Hey Rube: Blood Sport, the Bush Doctrine, and the Downward
        Spiral of Dumbness: Modern History from the Sports Desk*
        published (collection of ESPN columns).

Hunter and Warren Zevon shooting at Owl Farm

I N 1996 I told Hunter, in his language, in a speech, that I loved him. That year a poet and professor from Kentucky named Ron Whitehead contacted him about a Hunter S. Thompson tribute to be held in Louisville, Kentucky, Hunter's hometown. It would be held in the Memorial Auditorium in downtown Louisville. A number of his friends would pay tribute, either by speaking or in song. Hunter agreed to go, and began recruiting. Johnny Depp agreed to appear, along with Warren Zevon, Doug Brinkley, Roxanne Pulitzer, and musician David Amram. Bob Braudis, the sheriff of Pitkin County, would be bodyguard and road man, and Ron asked me to come as well to say a few words. I had never spoken in public before, and certainly not about Hunter. I had no idea what to write or how to write it. I borrowed a laptop from work and figured I'd write something on the plane, or in the hotel room.

I took a day off from work at the University of Colorado and joined Hunter and Bob in Denver, where we all flew to Louis-ville. Ron put us all up at the Brown Hotel, an elegant old place downtown. Hunter had a corner suite on the top floor overlook-ing the city, where he entertained a steady stream of people who had come for the event, including old friends from his child-hood, students from Ron Whitehead's classes, and the various presenters. That was the first night I met Johnny Depp, who had spent the last several months living in the basement at Owl Farm and shadowing Hunter in preparation for playing Raoul Duke in the movie *Fear and Loathing in Las Vegas*.

After dinner I went back to my room to write my speech. I was scared. What if my speech was bad? What if I froze? What if I couldn't come up with anything? I got a couple of sentences down, but finally gave up and went to bed, hoping for a clearer head in the morning.

With Hunter and Will on the John Deere tractor. Hunter was showing off for Will in the driveway at Owl Farm, 2001.

We went to the auditorium early the next afternoon for the light and sound check. While Warren Zevon sat at the piano and practiced, I sat on the low bleachers at the back of the stage and finished my speech on my laptop.

By seven p.m. the auditorium was packed. More than two thousand tickets had been sold and it was standing room only. Hunter's mother, Virginia Thompson, who lived her whole life in Louisville, was in the front row. Doug Brinkley kicked off the evening, followed by a series of speakers such as Roxanne Pulitzer. Harvey Sloane, the previous mayor of Louisville and a childhood friend, presented Hunter with a key to the city. Johnny Depp read from *Fear and Loathing in Las Vegas* in his recently acquired Hunter Thompson persona, and Warren Zevon performed several songs. David Amram played a variety of instruments, and a local college student read a poem she had written in honor of Hunter. The whole time he stood offstage, just behind the curtain, watching the performances, whooping now and then, and soaking up the tributes.

I was the final speaker, and as my time approached I became more and more nervous.

It didn't occur to me at the time how remarkable it was that Hunter was willing to let me speak at this event. He had no idea what I was going to say. This was a huge day for him, the troubled young man makes good and returns triumphant to his hometown, and he was letting me speak, and speak last. He trusted me.

Doug Brinkley introduced me, and I walked up to the podium, reminded myself to speak slowly, and began.

A week ago I received this opportunity to pay tribute to my father at this event. I was first very excited, as you can imagine. It is not every child who has the chance to honor his father in their lifetimes, or even in solitude. I am very fortunate. Thank you, Ron Whitehead, for putting this event together, and thank you all for coming.

A few days later, I started to get nervous. How on earth am I going to honor him? What can I say? I decided to start with the question I am most often asked, which is, "What was it like to have Hunter Thompson as your father?"

On one level, it is an empty question. It is like being anyone's son, it is unique. I have nothing to compare it to, I have one father and one childhood. What I can tell you, however, is what I learned from my father, what I respect and admire in him.

First of all, he is impossible to categorize or define. He is original. More than anyone I can think of, he crosses boundaries, he embodies more contradictions than any ten ordinary people. He is both a madman and southern gentleman, a prophet and a hooligan, an idealist and a cynic. He thrives on disruption, unpredictability, and thwarting expectation, yet is bound to social conventions.

Years ago he chastised me for not minding my manners and shaking someone's hand at the proper time, yet he will set off a roll of five thousand firecrackers in his best friend's bedroom at three a.m. I respect and admire, and sometimes fear, the way he lives moment to moment.

I appreciate his power and courage. My father is nothing if not powerful. He is like an extremely volatile chemical that illuminates with flashes of fire and thunder the lives of those who come in contact with him. He is not afraid, as I think most of us are, to make an impression. He makes us wake up and take notice. We may not like what we see, I don't think he cares at all what people LIKE—the important thing is that we wake up and take notice.

I have learned that the surface truth is rarely the real truth, and as a result I have become cynical about the motivations of corporations, politicians, and law enforcement. Above all, he makes me think and pay attention. He demands in everything that he does that you set aside your habits of perception and pay attention to what is happening right now, and deal with it. That's where the fun and excitement are, in not knowing what's going to happen.

I have learned to appreciate words. Whatever else brings you all here, I hope that you all recognize my father's genius for using the English language. He is an artist, which to me means he is a magician with words, he makes them express his vision of the world in a way that cannot be attained by study and effort and even practice, though he has done all these things. It is more than mechanical mastery, it is expressing the living essence of a scene or a person directly. A few years ago he sent me a three-volume set of the *Webster's Third New International Dictionary of the English Language,* bound in brown leather. That summed up, I think, the values he wished to convey to me. Though I have not inherited his magic, I have inherited a love of words and books and fine writing.

I learned to appreciate the beauty of guns and the thrill of shooting them. Anyone who has shot a large caliber pistol or a shotgun and felt the rush of so much raw power in your hand knows what I mean. I've spent many nights with Hunter cleaning shotguns and oiling pistols. I was shooting a .22 rifle by the age of ten, and at my engagement party a few years ago I shot with a twelve-gauge shotgun loaded with double-o buckshot, dead center, a propane canister attached to a can of gasoline, which made a spectacular fireball in the night outside Owl Farm. I was proud, and I know he was too.

I have learned to appreciate family and loyalty to one's friends. I have never seen a community closer than the one in Aspen that I grew up in and that Hunter helped to create and hold together. These people are serious about friendship, and whatever their flaws, inherent in being human, they protect each other. When there is legal trouble within or without, they come together and pool resources and support. When someone is going through difficult times, there are suddenly more invitations to dinner, to watch the football games, subtle invitations to talk and unload. If someone is done wrong by an outsider, then the offender finds himself on a collective blacklist.

I have learned to appreciate driving fast and following the fall line through a curve. I know the pleasure of driving a red 1973 Chrysler convertible with the top down on a sunny fall day. I love the adrenaline, focus, and vitality that come from riding a motorcycle at eighty miles per hour on a winding country road. These things I learned from Hunter.

I learned that some cops lie. This was a brutal and profoundly disturbing realization: Those in control are not necessarily trustworthy. More importantly, authority is not necessarily to be obeyed, and certainly not feared. There is always a way to challenge authority, either in the courtroom or in the media or in the voting booth. He has done all of them many times, and usually successfully. In other words, he believes that it is possible to change a situation for the better, even in the face of entrenched authority.

So what am I saying? I am proud of this man. I respect and admire his vitality, his courage, his insight, his perverse resistance to security and predictability, his deliberate disregard for propriety, his ability to make me see and think differently. Ultimately, I love and respect him because he really *lives,* for better or for worse, for richer or for poorer, he *lives* his life.

It wasn't a long speech, maybe five minutes. I remember how quiet it was in the auditorium just before I started to read, and then the sound of my own voice booming through the hall. Once I started to read, slowly, my nervousness evaporated and I felt an unfamiliar sense of calmness and intensity. When I finished, Hunter walked onto the stage from the wings where he had been watching with a fire extinguisher and blasted me a few times, which I took as a sign of his approval. He grabbed my shoulder and said, "Well done, man." That was it, nothing more. But it was enough.

With the event over, chaos erupted as hundreds of people surged onto the stage to find Hunter and thank him, or touch him, or get his autograph. One guy brought his book with him to be signed, and then realizing that he would not be able to penetrate the crowd around Hunter on the stage, came up to me and asked me to sign his book instead. I signed it, "In honor of my father." Hunter stood on the stage for a long time signing books and talking with fans. Then a fire broke out in the green room backstage and I heard a rumor that some fans got out of hand and began breaking furniture. Hunter escaped out the back door and into a limo, and I did not see him again until the next morning. I heard stories of him driving a car down sidewalks in downtown Louisville at high speed, a wall on one side and trees on the other, while Braudis hung on, white-knuckled. Bob said the next day that it was his last trip as Hunter's road man.

Our plane back to Colorado was in the afternoon. A few hours before our flight I found Hunter in his hotel room just waking up. As I was stuffing his clothes into his suitcase and Hunter was getting dressed, he said to me in an offhand way, "Don't kid yourself about the magic," referring to my speech. I will never forget those words.

That was the last time we ever talked about that night. It wasn't the last time he talked about it, though. Wayne Ewing, a documentary filmmaker, had shot the entire evening and made an edited version that he gave to Hunter. Hunter watched my speech over and over again, and each time he would have guests, he would make them watch the entire tape if they hadn't seen it already, and even if they had. That's when I understood how important that night had been to him. Of course he valued the affirmation from his hometown, the town he had left in disgrace forty years earlier, forced to either join the air force or go to jail while his wealthy friends went to Ivy League universities. That night some of those same people had come to pay him tribute, he had the key to the city, it was officially Hunter S. Thompson Day in Louisville, and the governor had appointed him a Kentucky colonel. He was vindicated.

Keith Richards, Jane Rose, Laila Nabulsi, and Hunter on the couch at Owl Farm. Hunter interviewed Keith in 1993.

But what mattered most to him were not those tributes, but my speech. It has taken me years to understand this. It meant much more than if I had just said, "I love you, Hunter." It was a public confirmation that I had forgiven him for his failures and transgressions as a father, that I admired him for the right reasons. I was proud of my father, and now everyone knew it.

I used to think that that was the night that Hunter stopped wondering if I loved and respected him. Now I see that he knew it before I stepped up to the microphone. Nevertheless, it made him very, very happy to hear it spoken in front of a couple of thousand people. He needed absolution from me, his child, his son, his blood and heir. It wasn't until after his death that I became conscious of this, but that didn't matter. I gave him what he needed when he was alive.

Three years later, I learned to show my love for him in a very

Grandpa Hunter, or "Ace" as he preferred to be called, with Will at the IBM Selectric in the Command Chair in the kitchen at Owl Farm

different way; Hunter endured two very difficult surgeries that pushed my patience and acceptance right up to my limits.

IN 1999, when Will was a little over one year old, I got a call from Deborah. She said that Hunter was going into the hospital for hip replacement surgery. He was sixty-two, and for the past several years he had been suffering from increasing hip pain. He rarely talked about it, but he took a lot of painkillers every day, and he didn't walk much. He would go from his bed to his Command Chair at the kitchen counter. There, within arm's reach, he had his typewriter, two telephones, the stereo, and about ten remote controls to operate the television and its associated devices, as well as the last several days' worth of newspapers, his medicines, the stove, the coffee machine, a copy of each of his books, small Macanudo cigars, a jarful of pens, and blank paper and stationery. For things beyond an arm's reach, like cooking, faxing, fixing drinks, getting newspapers, and so on, he relied on whoever was present, and there was nearly always somebody there. But this was not an acceptable situation to a man like Hunter. He had always been able to go where he wished, when he wished. His hip pain had greatly reduced his mobility, and he could no longer pretend that the pain was not agonizing.

And he hated hospitals. They were little more than prisons to him, with all their rules and restrictions. Hunter did not belong in a hospital. Finally, though, the pain was too much.

Jennifer, Will, and I went to see him a week or so before the operation. He showed us the hip joint, an extra-large version that the hospital had had to special-order for him. It was titanium and looked like a large, high-tech tent stake, the top of which had been bent to the side. It was a beautiful thing, shining and precisely made. He showed it to all his visitors. He described how the surgeon would saw off the top of his femur and replace it with this.

Deborah asked us to come and help take care of him at the hospital once the surgery was complete. The hospital was in Glenwood Springs, about forty miles from Aspen. We returned the day after the surgery and checked into the Cedar Lodge Motel a few blocks from the hospital.

We went to see Hunter and found him in a drugged sleep in a darkened room. Deborah was there. He looked old. The surgery had gone well, but the doctor was shocked at how little of the joint was left, that it was just a rough stump grinding into his hip bone. He had been "acting up," and earlier that day had grabbed a long steel pole that reached across the bed above him and thrown it at one of the nurses.

A normal person would sleep off the general anesthesia and then spend a few days in bed, in pain but generally conscious, while his body began to heal, then spend several days in physical therapy learning how to work with this new joint to undo some of the unconscious adaptations bodies make to minimize pain. This was not Hunter's plan.

The biggest problem was not his temperament, his dislike of rules and doctors, or his tantrums, it was alcohol. He and the surgeon had had a frank discussion about it before the surgery. Some doctors see a hospital visit as an opportunity to impose The Cure, a time for the patient to detoxify in a safe environment and start life anew, free of alcohol dependence. Hunter made it clear that he had no interest in The Cure. The surgeon accepted this and instructed the nurses to give him whiskey as part of his drug regimen. It actually appeared on the sheet that describes what drugs a patient should have when, and how much. It was something like "500 cc of whiskey every two hours or as needed." He had to have alcohol in his system all the time or he would go into withdrawal, which could be fatal given how much Hunter drank every day. The withdrawal came on swiftly. His last drink had been the night before. By the time he was out of surgery, withdrawal had begun.

Hunter became delirious, irrational, angry, confused—but most dangerous of all, the withdrawal caused him to forget to take his dose of alcohol, accelerating the withdrawal and the accompanying mental confusion.

So Hunter had to go through detox in a drug-induced coma to protect him, as well as those of us caring for him. Deborah, Heidi, and I worked in shifts throughout the day and night to keep an eye on him, to keep an eye on the doctors and nurses, and to reassure him if he woke up and wondered where in the hell he was.

It was scary, seeing my father in a coma, watching the doctors try to balance the speed of withdrawal with the problems caused by immobility: bedsores, weakened muscles, and pneumonia. He was completely vulnerable. His rage and willpower could not help him now. He was old, pale, and drawn, and a victim of his own disease.

It hit me hard then that the most dangerous drug for my father wasn't cocaine, it was alcohol. Hunter had never been a binge drinker or a stupid drunk. He was a maintenance drinker from the time he woke up to the time he went to bed. He didn't slur his words, or suddenly go into rages (no more than any other time), confess his deepest feelings, become syrupy sweet, or pass out on the couch; you could say he handled his liquor well. In fact, he had disdain for sloppy drunks. If a guest at Owl Farm showed signs of not being able to hold his or her liquor, he would become impatient with them, and eventually tell them to leave.

He survived the detox without any major problems, and finally the doctors weaned him off the sedatives. He woke up, irritable, in pain, but coherent. He was aware that he was in a hospital, and he wasn't happy about it. The detox had been the easy part. Now it got hard.

Being one of Hunter's caretakers in the hospital highlighted one of the dilemmas of loving him. I found myself in the position of being both advocate and warder, trying, with little success, to enforce the recommendations of the doctors because I wanted him to recover, while also enabling the very things that slowed down the healing process: cigarettes and booze.

For instance, the doctors and nurses explained to Hunter and to us, the caretakers, that he would have to limit his leg's range of movement for several months until his body had fully healed around the artificial joint. If he bent over too far too soon, he could pop the joint right out of the socket, which would be extremely painful and possibly require surgery again, and would force him to start the whole healing process over. I'd remind him sternly, "Don't bend so far! Remember, no more than ninety degrees!" At first he would grudgingly acquiesce, but he soon ignored me. Thankfully the joint stayed put and never popped out—someone might have lost a body part in the ensuing chaos of rage and pain that would have followed.

Then there was smoking. The doctor told us that it impedes healing by constricting blood vessels, and that it would be best if he stopped. Hunter had been smoking longer than he had been drinking, probably fifty years, and it was inconceivable that he would stop. Whenever the nurses weren't around, he would smoke in the room with the window open. Many times I ended up pushing him in a wheelchair to a position just outside the emergency room doors where there was an ashtray and a couple of newspaper dispensers. He would smoke a few cigarettes, read *The Denver Post* or the *Rocky Mountain News,* and then demand to be returned to his room.

It was a long week. He was irritable, unreasonable, sometimes mean, demanding, ungrateful, and complaining. I tried to be patient. It was summer, thankfully, so I was eventually able to take him outside and onto the lawn. I would bring him lunch, his cigarettes, and his newspapers, and we would sit under a little tree for a couple of hours until he was ready to go back inside. He had resumed drinking whiskey as soon as his mind cleared, and this was a relief because it was one more familiar thing for him in a thoroughly unfamiliar and inhospitable place.

After about a week Hunter had recovered to the point that he no longer needed the high-touch, frequent, and intrusive medical attention and could move to another room. He could only walk with the use of a walker, and then only a short distance, less than one hundred feet, before the exertion and the pain overcame his need for independence and he had to rest. But he was thoroughly sick of the hospital and wanted to go home. Nothing at Owl Farm, with its narrow doorways, steps, high stools, and slick tile floors, was suited to a cripple. It would be a disaster to bring him home, where he would be completely dependent on Deb, not just for the usual things, but now for his complete physical care as well. We argued with him, tried to make him understand how utterly impractical it was, and that he would have to work hard in physical therapy for at least a week before he could even consider going home. He was unmoved. He just wanted to go home. We finally persuaded him to at least spend a few days doing physical therapy. Though he was weak, he did well the first day, and we were optimistic that he would be strong enough in a few days to go home.

That was too long for Hunter. If his caretakers would not take him home, then his friends would. The next day, Jennifer, Will, and I were in his room. At Hunter's request, Jennifer had bought a tricycle for Will, along with a little helmet and Richard Scarry's classic, *What Do People Do All Day?* Will was riding the trike around the room, and he and Hunter were playing hoops with a little stuffed basketball and the trash can. Suddenly three giants appeared, the three biggest men Hunter knew, all of them well over six feet tall and two hundred pounds: Oliver, Bob Braudis, and Ed Bastian, Buddhist scholar, filmmaker, and local entrepreneur. They had come to take him home. After some friendly chitchat, they hoisted Hunter in their arms and took him to Owl Farm. With difficulty they carried him up the steps (no railing) and to his (low) bed, where they left him (with no wheelchair and no walker). Being at home also allowed him to begin his cocaine use again, which further slowed down the healing process.

It had been well over a week and I had to return to work, so at this point Jen, Will, and I returned to Denver. There was a limit to how much I could do, both in terms of time off and psychologically. I was angry, tired, and emotionally worn out. I wanted to go home too.

Even now, every time we drive through Glenwood Springs on the way to Owl Farm, I feel a vague sick feeling and a desire get through the town as quickly as possible.

Yet, thank god I had been there. This would not have happened ten years earlier. He wouldn't have wanted me there, and I wouldn't, couldn't, have done it. I wouldn't have had the patience, and he would not have trusted me. By allowing me to help take care of him, Hunter demonstrated his trust in me. By showing up and spending my two weeks of vacation in a goddamn hospital and putting up with his foul moods and unreasonable demands, I validated that trust.

Jennifer, Will, and I came to visit a month or two later and found Hunter to be noticeably calmer and happier than we had seen him in years. He was less irritable, more likely to smile, and was generally a nicer person to be around. We attributed this to the absence of chronic pain.

Afterward, we rarely talked about the surgery, and it turned out that he remembered little of it, but he knew I had been there and stuck it out. And I knew that I could be there with him when he was weak, vulnerable, and not on his best behavior. We had survived the test.

Four years later, in 2003, we went through it all again. I thought it would be just like the previous experience, but this was much

With Hunter, Will, and Jen in the kitchen at Owl Farm, 1999. Once Hunter got over the reality of being a grandfather, he was a doting one.

more difficult. Before he had been demanding and unreasonable. This time he was cruel.

His hip was no longer bothering him, but now his lower back was causing him great pain. As with his hip, he avoided walking as much as possible, and when he did walk, he hunched over to alleviate the pressure on the nerves in his back. He began using a rolling office chair as a kind of walker in the house. Driving became intolerable because even a small bump in the road was extremely painful, and it was hard for him to get in and out of his Jeep Grand Cherokee.

Hunter had become more reclusive over the years, preferring to stay home and have people visit him. It gradually became a huge ordeal to prepare to leave the house even for a few hours. This meant letting Hunter know several hours beforehand that he had to start getting ready. He would find a thousand ways to procrastinate. One trick he used when he really didn't want to leave the house was to go to the bathroom, and then sneak down the hall to the bedroom. After half an hour we'd go check on him and find the bathroom door open and Hunter in bed again. There was getting dressed, and then preparing for travel. You'd think he was going away for a week—the bag had to be packed with all the essentials he might need, including cigarettes, drugs, whiskey, cookies, a flashlight, host gifts, practical jokes, and anything else he thought he might need while away from home for a few hours. Throughout this preparation he was certain to lose his temper at least a few times, but that was just part of the process.

I'm sure that his back pain was a big factor in his growing reclusiveness. He did not want people to see him moving like a cripple. Much better that people see him seated in the Command Chair, his throne. He also needed to be close to the bathroom, because one of the symptoms of pinched nerves in the lower back is a lessened ability to control one's bowels. Incontinence is also a symptom of long-term alcoholism.

Finally the pain and inability to move comfortably led him to agree to back surgery.

The success of the hip operation made him more willing the second time around, and this time he involved me early in the process. I was honored and apprehensive.

He had picked the hospital, the Steadman-Hawkins Clinic in Vail, a couple hours from Aspen. The clinic was known for fixing up famous athletes' orthopedic injuries. Hunter asked me to meet him and Deb in Vail for his first consultation with the back surgeon who would be performing the operation. I agreed.

It was a surreal interview. As part of the information-gathering process, the doctor asked Hunter questions about his drug and alcohol use. He explained that he needed accurate information to determine the risks of surgery. Hunter downplayed it all. When the surgeon asked how much he drank each day, he said several glasses. When he asked about cocaine use, Hunter said it was minimal. When he asked about marijuana use, Hunter said it was infrequent. Deborah and I knew differently. Hunter was uncomfortable but remained calm as we adjusted his earlier estimates substantially upward. A couple of drinks a day? Closer to a fifth of whiskey. Minimal cocaine use? More like several grams a day. Infrequent pot smoking? Only if you consider several times a week infrequent. On top of that, he was a chain-smoker. It was a rare moment indeed when Hunter did not have a lit cigarette either between his lips, in his fingers, or in an ashtray, along with the signature cigarette holder, the TarGard. On the ledge behind the kitchen sink at Owl Farm there was always a glass filled with TarGard filters and some liquid that dissolved the tar. I wonder how many vats, how many fifty-five-gallon drums of tar he

avoided inhaling over his fifty-odd years of smoking because of
those filters.

The doctor took it all in stride. He explained that alcohol and
smoking were the two biggest impediments to healing, and that
Hunter would be best served by abstaining from, or at least cutting back on, booze and cigarettes. Hunter replied that he was
(still) not interested in The Cure or in quitting smoking. If the
surgeon had a problem with that then Hunter needed another
doctor. The doctor explained that his concerns were purely medical, and that Hunter would be allowed to drink before and after
surgery. This was familiar territory to Deb and me. We very
much did not want a replay of Hunter's involuntary detoxifica-
tion in Glenwood.

Afterward, Hunter and I stopped for a late lunch at the Half
Moon café, the closest thing to a dive bar in Vail. He had to
take a piss something fierce, so he stood up behind the open
driver's side door and let go right there in the parking lot. I attributed it to Hunter being Hunter. It was embarrassing, but I was
used to being uncomfortable around Hunter in public. It was no
stranger than sitting next to him while he discreetly snorted a bit
of cocaine in a restaurant, or ordered whiskey and beer for breakfast. Now I know that this was because of his back and perhaps
his alcoholism, that he was losing control of his bladder. If he
hadn't peed right there, he would have pissed his pants, and that
would have been a terrible humiliation for him, even with me.

Hunter got an MRI of his back, and I went with him again
a couple of weeks later for a second conference with his doctor,
who explained the problem, spinal stenosis. This is a fancy medical term that means a plugged-up spinal cord channel, which
put a lot of pressure on the spinal cord itself, causing great pain

as well as other problems since the nerves were not able to relay their signals back and forth reliably. There was also a vertebra that had slipped out of position, putting yet more pressure on the delicate spinal cord. It was a simple operation, he said. Open up the back, clean out the scum with a brush, pull the vertebra back into position and fasten it there with some screws and bits of metal, then close him up. Wouldn't take more than a few hours. He said Hunter's age was the greatest risk, but that his chances of a completely successful operation were better than 50 percent, especially if he cut back on the booze and cigarettes to give his back a chance to heal. He was very matter-of-fact, confident, and patient as we asked many questions.

Like the doctor, Hunter talked about the operation in mechanical terms. He said it was simply fixing a machine whose parts were beginning to wear out. It was like taking a car in for a valve job—open up the engine, clean things up, replace a few worn parts, and put it back together. The key was in having a smart and experienced mechanic who knew what to do and what not to do.

I met Hunter in Vail a third time for a cardiac stress test. A heart doctor hooked him up to some machines and injected him with something that speeded his heart rate up to 140 or 150 beats per minute, while Hunter was lying perfectly still on the bed. After the test was complete, the doctor said his heart was in perfect shape for a guy his age, and that he had nothing to worry about.

Finally, the surgery itself was scheduled. Hunter was to show up the night before, spend the night in the hospital, and have the operation early the next morning. He would be out of the hospital in three to five days if all went well. "If all went well," that terrifying caveat. I don't think anything ever went according to a plan in Hunter's life—that is, when he had a plan at all. This time wouldn't be any different.

Jennifer, Will, and I met Hunter that night at the hospital. It was off-season in Vail and the place was practically empty. He had a room at the end of the hall where he could carry on without disrupting the handful of other patients on the floor. Deborah was already there. Hunter drank his usual whiskey and water up until midnight, which was the cutoff. The surgery was scheduled for seven a.m., and by noon he would be drinking again. Twelve hours without alcohol was well within his safety zone. We said good night and promised to be there as soon as he came out of surgery.

The four of us were staying at the Evergreen Lodge next door to the hospital. Over the next two weeks we wore our own path out the back door of the lodge, through the parking lot, and up the side stairs to the second floor of the hospital. When we arrived the next morning we went to the hospital. He was in surgery; it was going well. As soon as it was finished, he was wheeled into post-op, a mini-ward just off the operating theater. I went in to see him when he woke up and he already had a fifth of Chivas Regal cradled in his arm. I was very relieved to see he had already had a sip of whiskey.

I understood when I saw him that my strong, terrifying father was vulnerable. He had been on an operating table, deep in a sleep that he could not wake from, so deep that he could not feel the doctors cutting open his back, grabbing hold of his very spine, reaching in with tools and drills and bits of metal. He was completely at their mercy, completely and utterly vulnerable. I imagine him now like a doll or a mannequin, flopped on his stomach on the operating table, helpless. In that post-op room I saw that for all his power, he inhabited the body of an older man, and during that surgery his body could have given up on him.

But there he was, groggy, with his bottle of whiskey, now being wheeled into one of the acute care rooms that I got to know very well over the next couple of weeks. Hunter's spirit was dragging his tired and worn body along the trail, saying, "Come on, just a bit farther, just around that next bend. Come on," and it acquiesced, yes, a bit farther, okay. Let's see what's there.

It was a good room. A large window overlooked the creek that runs through Vail. It was early summer and everything was green, the grass, the trees, the fields, and the mountain hillside across the stream. The weather was cool and the sun was bright in the deep blue Colorado sky. The nurses hooked him up to the various monitors and he slept. That night he was awake and was strangely calm. He laughed, he was gentle. That fierce edge had abated. The doctor had told us that unlike the hip surgery, back surgery provided almost instant relief. We were all excited and relieved. No withdrawal this time, thank god. Hunter ate a bit, and drank a bit, and slept again. A few more days and he could go home.

But the next day things began to go wrong. He was delirious and angry. He wouldn't eat. He went in and out of sleep. His doctor told us he had begun withdrawal. He had had some whiskey, yes, but not enough, and now it was too late. Just like last time, once the process started, he wouldn't drink any alcohol. Hunter's life was full of irony and paradox, and this was one of them—he wouldn't drink even a sip of whiskey. Just as in Glenwood, his doctor decided to put him into a drug-induced coma to minimize the impact of the withdrawal. They loaded him up with lorazepam and put him to sleep. The doctor gave him alcohol intravenously, but it wasn't enough. Could they increase the alcohol dose, we asked? Apparently not. The highest concentration available for IV use would not be enough for Hunter.

The days began to blur together. Just like last time, there were complications because of the length of time he was lying in bed; he was getting water in his lungs; he needed machines to keep the blood and lymph moving in his legs. Though unconscious, he would cough up thick, yellowish green mucus, so we all took turns vacuuming his mouth with a little tube. Meanwhile the doctor was very, very slowly reducing his lorazepam, trying to balance the withdrawal against the dangers of having him asleep and immobile. The doctor also started him on Haldol, a powerful antipsychotic drug used to treat delirium, along with acute psychosis, severe behavioral disorders, and borderline personality disorder.

After a week or so he started to wake. At first, he was too weak and groggy to be irritable, but as he became gradually more aware of his surroundings and the nature of his captivity, he became angry and demanding. He wanted to go home. This time we told him no, he was not going home yet. He got angry and accused me of abandoning him. He got mean. One day we were taking him for a walk along the creek in a wheelchair. Sheriff Braudis had come down for the afternoon and was pushing the chair, and I was walking alongside. Hunter wanted something and he couldn't have it. I remember his eyes got small in his face; they reminded me of pig eyes, they became hard and small and his face kind of puckered up so that there was nothing but hatred and cruelty there. He said something to me, I can't remember exactly what, but that was it.

I walked away, not caring what happened to him. I was furious and hurt. To hell with him. I had known it wouldn't be easy, but I didn't expect this viciousness, this foulness, this deliberate hurt.

After that, I avoided him. I still talked to his doctor to understand how he was doing, but I didn't want to talk to him. I wanted
to hit him hard, I wanted to hurt him. Here I was in a replay
of childhood, trapped with this savage bastard, unable to leave,
unable to change him, enduring it until he was well enough to be
sent home and out of my life for a while.

Over the years, I would occasionally have dreams about Hunter
and myself. For a long time they were terrifying dreams in which
he was a giant mad with rage, so angry at me that I thought he
would kill me, and in my terror, and then later my fury, I would
beat on him with my fists, crying and screaming, but with no
effect. His rage was volcanic. I could not escape him, nor could I
hurt him. He was unstoppable and he wanted to kill me.

Then I would wake up, shaken, frightened, and reflect on the
marvelous nature of the unconscious, how such powerful and
primitive feelings can remain hidden from our own consciousness. I was amazed at how frightening he was to me still.

Starting several years before his death, I began to have, in addition to these dreams of the murderous giant, dreams in which I
learned that Hunter was dead. Though my dreams usually evaporate during the transition to full wakefulness, I can still remember my feeling of utter despair, as if the whole world was ending
and there was no way I could go on. I would have these dreams a
few times a year. I would wake from these dreams sad, frightened
at the power my father had over me, marveling again at what was
so deeply hidden inside myself so that it took a dream to show
me how much my father meant to me.

By the end of the second week he was well enough, and mean
enough, to demand to leave the hospital. He threatened to sue
the doctor and the hospital for keeping him against his will,
while the doctor threatened to eject him if he didn't calm down

and stop verbally abusing the nurses. At one point he tried to get into a wheelchair so he could leave the hospital by himself in a cab, but he couldn't even get out of bed.

Finally there came the day when Hunter was determined to go home. It had been two weeks, and it was clear that he would find a way to get home that day, with or without the help of his caretakers. I was no longer talking to him at this point, I wouldn't even go in his room, but I arranged for a taxi van to come and take him home. When the van arrived, a few hospital staff members loaded him into the car, and off he went.

Jennifer, Will, and I went home. I was still angry at him. After about a week, I sent him a fax demanding an apology for his rotten, stinking behavior, and that until he did so I had no intention of seeing him.

A couple of nights later he called, very late as usual, and left a message on our answering machine saying he was sorry, and thanks for all my help. To get an apology, however brief, was a very big deal indeed. It was the first time in my whole life that he apologized to me.

He and I talked about it a couple of months later and he said he didn't remember a thing during that two weeks. He remembered going into the hospital the night before, and then he remembered being home. He didn't remember what he had said to me or threatened to do (though Deborah reminded him) but he had apologized anyway.

I was that important to him, the murderous giant who tried to kill me in my nightmares and the father whose death I would grieve deeply. I had to forgive him because I loved him and I needed him.

• • •

ONE OF THE WAYS we built the bridge between us during this time of reconciliation was through swimming together. Hunter loved to swim. He mentioned it in his letters from the '50s and '60s, secretly slipping into someone's pool in the middle of the night, swimming silently, in no hurry, then slipping out again, his presence unknown to the pool's owner. He didn't swim for sport, he didn't don the goggles and cap and do fifty or a hundred laps. He swam for fun, for the peace, the darkness, and the easy, graceful movement in the water.

He never had a pool at Owl Farm. He did have his neighbor's pool, though. He had an understanding with Stranahan, who many years ago added a lap pool to his house a few miles up the road. Hunter was free to use the pool between midnight and dawn, or until the family began to stir, whichever came first.

In the '90s, when we were well into our reconciliation period, I went to that pool with him many times. As it had been in his youth, swimming was not about sport or fitness, it was a kind of meditation. He often went alone or with a woman, and very rarely, if ever, with another man. It was a privilege for me to join him in this late-night ritual.

We never left before midnight. First, we'd undress and put on thick, long bathrobes, no swimsuits, and then assemble the kit bag. This was a big black gym bag that carried all the swimming necessities, such as tequila, dark chocolate, Pepperidge Farm Milano cookies, a few waterproof flashlights, cigarettes, a few lighters, towels, a sharp knife, and a couple of grapefruits. It would be at least forty-five minutes from the time we first began to prepare to the time we backed the Jeep out of the garage. It's hard to say why it took so long. Sometimes Hunter would have some very specific item—a particular floating flashlight—that he had to have, or a particular lighter. Sometimes he would sit at the counter in the kitchen and search for something that he might realize he needed once he saw it, like a rubber rat, or fake vomit, or a bloody hand, something that he could leave as an unexpected gift for George's family in the pool room.

Eventually, we'd step into our Sorels, the heavy winter boots lined with felt, and get in the Jeep. Sometimes I would drive and sometimes he would. He was very particular about driving and nervous when he was not behind the wheel, so I took it as a sign of his confidence in me that he would sometimes ask me to drive. It seems like it was always winter when I went swimming with him. The Stranahans' house was up the valley, at the end of the paved road. The road continues beyond, but it is a narrow dirt road that becomes perilous as it approaches Lenado, the old lumber mill town a good ten miles further on.

We'd drive to the turnoff and head up a small valley, up the mile-long driveway, past the barn and guesthouse where Hunter, Sandy, and I had lived when we first moved to Woody Creek back in 1966, until we reached the main house. In back there was a narrow extension to the house that contained the lap pool. We'd pull up close to the house, but not so close as to wake the family, and turn off the engine. We'd turn on our flashlights, gather up the towels and kit bag, and step carefully through the deep snow to the sliding glass doors, which were never locked, a remnant of the rural ethic that dictated that you never locked your car at night and usually left the keys under the front seat. When I was a child we never locked the doors at night either. It was only after Hunter became well known enough to draw a steady trickle of uninvited visitors that he began to lock the doors of the house.

The pool room was dark, humid, and warm, like a greenhouse. There were windows along the full length of each long wall and skylights in the roof. We'd drop the kit bag by the steps into the pool and Hunter would press the button that would quietly roll up the pool cover. He'd throw a couple of floating, waterproof flashlights into the water to provide the only faint illumination—we never turned on the lights, that would have spoiled it completely—and then we'd shed the robes and get in the warm water.

If it was a clear night, we could see the stars through the sky-lights. There were thousands of them, with more appearing every minute as our eyes adjusted to the darkness. With the lights off in the pool room, at three a.m., at the top of a valley in Woody Creek, far from any city, the Milky Way stood out clearly and immediately. There were so many stars that it was difficult to pick out the familiar constellations among the myriad dots of light.

When I started swimming with him, he was suffering from first hip pain, then back pain. I realize now that this was one reason we parked so close to the pool—it was painful and risky for him to walk on an uneven, slippery surface. The pool gave him, in addition to the almost womblike warmth and darkness, the physical relief of removing the weight of his body from his legs and lower back. He would swim from one end to the other slowly and gracefully, sometimes using a backstroke, sometimes a breaststroke, maybe a bit of the crawl now and then. I never saw him calmer than at the pool. He said little, and when he did, he talked in almost a whisper, as if he was in a church, his own kind of church.

After a half hour or so, he would climb out of the pool and root around in the kit bag for a treat, maybe a bar of good dark chocolate, and we would share it. He would usually sit on the edge of the pool and I would stay in. Though he brought ciga-rettes and booze, he didn't smoke in the pool room. If he had anything to drink at all, it was just a shot of tequila. Afterward he would return to his slow and quiet swimming.

I tried to talk to him sometimes, thinking that this was our opportunity to have a meaningful father-son dialogue, the kind that I craved and thought we needed, but it never turned out that way. I would ask him questions—about Owl Farm, about his old friends—and he would answer briefly and go silent. Later I understood that the most important thing was spending this time together, whether we talked or not. After an hour or more Hunter would say it was time to go. We'd put our robes on, pack up the kit bag, making sure we had left nothing behind, and then grab the rope on the pool cover and slowly pull it back into place. It was understood that we were to leave it as we found it, as if we had never been there. Then we'd put on our Sorels again and walk back to the Jeep.

We talked very little, if at all, on the way back home. Speech would have been an intrusion. About halfway down the Stranahans' driveway there was a tiny graveyard where the original settlers of that valley were buried, just a couple of headstones surrounded by an old wrought-iron fence, and Hunter would always stop next to it, roll down the window, throw a couple of quarters over the top of the car into the graveyard, and then roll up the window and drive on. It was a part of the ritual.

My father had a superstitious temperament. He found comfort in ritual, as I do. He wasn't religious in a conventional sense, but he believed very strongly in an inherent moral order and in the concept of righteousness, and he believed in unseen forces that enforced that order. When he tossed the coins into the graveyard, he did it because he believed it was important to express his gratitude to those spirits who had made those late-night swims possible. He also knocked on wood to avoid jinxing a favorable outcome, and wore jewelry as talismans, not decoration. He wore an emerald pendant around his neck that was endowed with powers of protection. Exactly what those powers were, I didn't know, but he needed that pendant. He once considered giving it to me, and chose not to, because he felt he still needed it. His most powerful talisman, however, the one I believe is imbued with some of his power and essence, was the medallion.

In many of the photos, he is wearing a silver medallion that had been given to him in the late '60s by Oscar Acosta, the activist Chicano lawyer and model for Hunter's sidekick in *Fear and Loathing in Las Vegas,* and one of a small number of men whom Hunter respected and, I think, somewhat feared. He didn't wear it every day, only for special occasions. The rest of the time it hung on a lamp next to the Command Chair in the kitchen, where he would see it every day. In the photos from the 1970 Aspen sheriff's campaign, he is wearing the medallion. In portraits, he is wearing the medallion. He didn't wear it at home, or out to parties, though, and he certainly never allowed anyone else to wear it.

I now wear that medallion for events where I want to invoke Hunter's presence, or when I am acting as his representative. I wore it to Ed Bradley's funeral in 2006. Ed was another member of that small circle of men whom Hunter respected deeply. Ed was his equal, and Hunter did not have many equals in the realm of personal power. Unlike nearly every man in Hunter's life, Ed made it clear that when he came to visit, he was not approaching the throne to pay homage, he came as an equal, and expected to be treated as such. If Hunter had been alive when Ed died, he would have been at the funeral to honor his dear friend. But

Hunter was gone, so Ed's widow invited me as a representative of my father and their friendship. I wore the medallion with pride and humility: pride that I was representing my father, humility because I was representing my father.

Others recognized the power of the medallion. In 2007, Hunter's close friend from the 1970s, Tom Benton, was dying of cancer in a Denver hospital. Jennifer and I went to visit him daily for the few weeks he was there. He was often delirious or asleep, but one day he recognized me, and he saw the medallion around my neck. It seemed right to wear it to see Tom. He reached up and held the medallion between his fingers, smiled a bit, and nodded, as if greeting an old friend. Later, I asked him if there was anything I could get for him, and he said, "Give me the medallion." I couldn't do it, though, not even to lend it to him, not even for Tom. I know that if I had been able to ask Hunter what to do, he would have said something like, "Fuck no! Give him anything else, but not that. It is yours now, and only yours." It is bound to me now, until I give it to Will, a long time from now.

Hunter was superstitious about his actions. He called himself a Road Man for the Lords of Karma. He used that expression several times, most recently the night before he died. I don't know exactly what he meant by that, but I know he wasn't joking. He took seriously the idea that evil actions bear evil fruit, and that this is not a matter of psychology, but is a universal law. How he reconciled this with the harm that he inflicted on people around him, on my mother, on me, on countless women, on cabbies, bartenders, waiters, editors, hotel maids, journalists, audience members, and anyone else who encountered his rage, I don't know. Maybe it all balanced out, the good he did and the harm he did, because he did a tremendous amount of good. He also spoke and wrote of reincarnation. Maybe he was serious about this. Maybe he feared he would be reincarnated as a three-legged dog with the mange in a garbage slum in Brazil, as he once wrote. Or maybe knew he would return as a crazy bodhisattva, to tell the truth and shake us out of our complacency. It is said that when the Tibetan Dalai Lama dies, he is reincarnated not long afterward somewhere else in Tibet. A group of high lamas goes in search of him, based on visions received during meditation, and when they find a candidate, they present him with things owned by the previous Dalai Lama mixed in with other objects. The true reincarnation identifies unerringly those objects that had once belonged to him. Perhaps someday I will encounter a young boy who will recognize this medallion as his, and then I will tell him all about who he had been and all that he did.

What I do know is that when Hunter tossed those coins into the graveyard after a midnight swim he wasn't figuratively thank-

Hunter and Tom Benton on the porch at Owl Farm

ing those spirits, he was making an offering with sincerity and faith, just like the Greeks burned the flesh of animals, and a Catholic priest holds the host before him in consecration during a mass. Maybe he was thanking them at least in part for helping to bring us together in that mysterious and indirect way. In that way, the birth of my own son, Will, also helped to bring us together.

The birth of Will changed my life completely. I expected that. What I did not expect is how it changed my relationship with my father, and how important my son was to Hunter.

When Jennifer was about three months pregnant, we drove up to Woody Creek to tell Hunter and Deb. We didn't tell them why we were coming, it was just a normal visit. We got there in the evening, as we usually did, and Hunter was just waking up, sitting in his Command Chair. That morning he was groggy and silent, reading the paper and gradually reengaging with the waking world.

It was just the four of us, Hunter, Deb, Jennifer, and me, and it was good to be together. This was rare. Most of the time when we arrived during this period between Will's birth and Deb's forced departure several years later, there were visitors. It could be Oliver, it could be a few neighborhood friends over to watch a football game, it could be an out-of-town visitor, or a lovely, young, so-called writing assistant, or a couple of lawyers strategizing with Hunter about how to handle the latest crisis or local political battle. The time when he was fresh from sleep was special because it meant we had his full attention, undiluted by distractions or drugs, whether that was weed, LSD, hash, too much whiskey at the end of two days without sleep, or some other substance that took him away from us.

We told them that Jen was having a baby. Deb was, of course, thrilled. Hunter was quiet. He probably nodded, muttered some words of congratulation, and then went back to reading the paper, though as always keenly aware of everything that was happening around him. What he was thinking I don't know, but I suspect it was the sudden realization that he was no longer a young man, or even a vigorous middle-aged man, but that he was now an elder, a grandfather. He continued reading and we talked about the usual things: politics, neighborhood news, anything interesting at my work. After a couple of hours he asked me to go down into the basement and bring up a bentwood rocking chair from the laundry room. I brought it up and he had me set it in the kitchen. The rocker was to be Jen's baby-nursing chair. He told her to sit, and when she tried to get up, he told her to sit down again. He had her sitting in that chair from time to time all weekend, practicing how she was going to take care of his grandson.

Later that night, or more accurately early the next morning, around four or five a.m., since we were on Hunter's time now, we went next door to the cabin to sleep, and found on the bed a sling, a maternity nightgown, and a rag doll. Deb had apparently been trolling the Aspen used stores for baby items, and it was now evident that they had been expecting this announcement.

Sunday we were to drive back to Boulder. Usually we would plan to leave in the afternoon, and between Hunter's schedule and the long good-bye, we would end up leaving around nine or ten p.m. This time, though, Hunter was up by late morning, and suggested that we go to lunch in Basalt. He generally disliked leaving the house, preferring that people come to him, and he especially didn't care for restaurants because of HST fans, smoking restrictions, and in general any rules that prevented him from doing exactly as he liked.

The fact that he wanted to go to a restaurant, and bring Oliver, meant that this was a very big deal. When we were seated, Hunter ordered a glass of milk for Jennifer. She was not a milk drinker, and she protested, but Hunter insisted. Just like with the rocker, she was going to take care of his grandson properly, and he wasn't asking her, he was telling her.

Leaving that afternoon was hard, harder than usual. It was downright sentimental, Hunter and Deb taking us to lunch to celebrate our announcement, and his concern for Jen. I did not expect this, not from Hunter, and I was overwhelmed by it.

HE MAY HAVE ACCEPTED that he was a grandfather among those very closest to him, but he wasn't enthusiastic about letting other people know. A couple of months later we came up for Christmas and were preparing to go to a dinner party with Hunter and a few of his friends, including Jimmy Buffett and Ed Bradley. Jennifer asked Hunter what she should wear, and he said, "Something that hides the fact that you're pregnant."

We arrived at Buffett's house, and as soon as Jennifer walked in the door, everybody knew. Jimmy said with a big smile, "So Hunter, you're going to be a grandfather!" Everyone was excited and made a big deal of it. During dinner both Jimmy and Ed teased him about it, and began discussing whether he would be a reluctant or a doting grandfather. They both agreed that he would be a doting grandfather. The worst was past, his friends now knew. From then on he did not hesitate. He was proud.

The existence of my son was still an abstract thing to me. To Jennifer, carrying this growing weight daily, feeling her body change, it was an undeniable reality, but to me, the fact of a child was not quite real, even though we were planning and talking to him inside Jen's belly. The day we went to get a sonogram made him very real.

It must have been around seven months. It was an incredible thing to see on that little black-and-white screen, full of static, the shape of a little human being, and the most magical was watching the screen as we went on a tour of his body. The doctor told us it was a boy. We saw inside Will's tiny skull, and then his spine, with its soft core surrounded by the hard vertebrae. We saw inside his heart, saw the chambers pumping. It was fascinating and disturbing, and it made Will, William Hunter Winkel Thompson, my son, real.

But not as real as his emergence into the world. We drove to the Boulder Community Hospital around six p.m. on a March evening in 1998. Jennifer's labor was long and difficult, so that the doctor had to drag Will out with a little suction hat and two huge spoons, but then he popped out, long, wet, skinny, and crying. The doctor put him on Jen's stomach, put two clips on his umbilical cord, and asked me if I wanted to cut it. I said yes, and he handed me the scissors. I can still feel the sensation as the blades touched the cord, the slight resistance, and then it was done. The nurse wrapped him in a blanket and handed him to me, and I held him tightly, amazed and quietly joyful. There were friends and relatives in the room, but I would not give him up except to Jennifer. When the nurses came for him to do their rituals of measuring, weighing, and so on, I was with him the whole time, holding him whenever I could, at least keeping my hand on him. It was over quickly and he returned to Jennifer's breast. A few hours later we were moved to a little room where we could sleep, and the two of us lay on the bed with this tiny, wrinkled, beautiful boy between us. After a few hours, we decided that we were better off at home. By three p.m. that afternoon we were driving our brand-new baby boy home, all wrapped in blankets and tucked into a baby seat.

It hit me hard that moment when I held Will for the first time. I loved him immediately and completely. I didn't love my son because he was beautiful, or healthy, or because of his name or his hair color. I loved him because I did, I had to. My son needed love and I had to love him because he was my son. That is all there was to it. The love comes first. As he grows, he gives me reasons to admire and respect him for what he does, but the love that was there in the beginning, unearned and without justification or condition, persists.

It seemed obvious then that to doubt a father's love, that instinctual and powerful embrace of love, would be to doubt some undeniable physical fact of our lives, like doubting the ocean tides, or the sun.

A few days later I called Hunter. I told him that I understood now how much a father loves his son, and that I was sorry that I had doubted his love before. It was suddenly so clear to me that a father must love his son.

He didn't say much, but I didn't need him to say anything, I just wanted him to hear me. He said something like, "Yes. Good. That's true." I told him I loved him, and I hung up.

I suddenly had a completely new perspective on my father. Of course he loved me. Yet this wasn't a Hollywood movie where the main character has an epiphany, the clouds roll back to reveal a smiling sun, and they live happily ever after. That's not how it works in my experience. It's more like fits and starts, a few steps forward, a few steps back, a flash of insight, and then back into the darkness until the next flash briefly illuminates the landscape. Thank god for those flashes, though, they keep me from walking in circles and giving up, despairing of ever seeing things clearly, even for a second.

So it was with this insight. It didn't resolve everything between my father and me completely and forever. What it did do, though, is give a starting place I could go back to. If I ever seriously wondered if my father loved me, and I did, I could go back to this and remember, of course he loves me. He must, he can't help it. He just has to. Just like I have to love Will. And it helped. It helps.

When Will was four months old, we brought him to Owl Farm to meet Hunter and Deb for the first time, and they organized a party in Will's honor for that weekend. The evening we arrived, though, it was another of those special times with no visitors and no distractions. Hunter was the picture of the doting grandfather. Sitting in his Command Chair, he held Will in his lap. He was gentle and patient, and Will, who would only let Jennifer, me, and Wendy, a good friend of ours, hold him without crying, sat quietly. Some men hold babies awkwardly, as if they don't want to hold them too close, or they're afraid they might break them. Hunter held Will easily, as if he were used to having babies on his lap. He talked to him, let him explore his breakfast on the plate on the counter, and held his tiny fingers. He showed Will the IBM Selectric typewriter that was always on the counter in front of him. He enfolded Will in an aura of warmth and concern. Hunter turned on the typewriter, and Will hit the keys. A couple of weeks later we got the sheet of Will's first typing in the mail.

While Will was sitting on his lap, playing with the typewriter, Hunter said, "I recognize this boy." I think Will recognized his grandfather as well. The next day during Will's party, Hunter was outside on the front porch, and Jennifer stepped outside carrying Will, who was crying, no doubt overwhelmed by the rush of stimuli and unfamiliar faces. Hunter reached and said, "Here, give him to me." This was madness. I could rarely calm him down once he got started crying, certainly Hunter would only make it worse. Jen handed him over, though, and Will suddenly stopped crying.

I'm not angry at Hunter very often about his suicide. I am angry, though, that he did not stay around for Will. His body was falling apart, he could barely walk, his new marriage seemed like a complete disaster, he couldn't concentrate long enough to write more than a few sentences, and his few, true friends were dying off. But what about his grandson? What about Will? It still makes me sad, as I write this years later, that they got to spend so little time together. Maybe it's my own sadness too. I miss my father very much still.

Hunter was remarkably patient with Will, but his self-restraint was not perfect. Football and basketball games were a vital part of his week, and though he liked having company during the games, there were rules that had to be observed. The most important rule was that while the game was on, side conversations must be quiet and discreet. Hunter would let people know in clear terms that their jabber was unwelcome and that they could either shut up or move to another room. Persistent violators were not invited back.

This was all very well for adults, but it was not reasonable for small children such as his grandson. While Jennifer and I watched the game, Will would play on the floor in the kitchen, and sometimes he would cry, or screech, or drop something. One time Hunter turned to Will and said something like, "Be quiet, you little bastard!" Jennifer glared at him and said, "Hunter, don't you dare talk to your grandson like that!," picked up Will, and went next door to the cabin. Hunter looked abashed and angry, and said nothing. I said later to him, "Hunter, he's a small child. He doesn't know what he's doing, and you can't yell at him like that." He may have grunted, but that was all. However, not long afterward he called Jen next door, apologized, and asked her to bring Will back over. It was a rare thing to get an apology like that.

That's how it was with Hunter. He could restrain himself for a while, and he tried very hard when we were there, but beyond a certain point he couldn't, or wouldn't, control himself, and if we hadn't left already, it was then time to go. We had worked out these compromises over many years without ever discussing them. We would come to visit almost monthly. When I was there, I would accept things like his schedule, which meant staying up until dawn a couple days in a row, and accept his drinking and drug use. In return, he would try his utmost to refrain from unreasonable outbursts at me, or asking me to fix his drinks for him. Sometimes the bargain broke down. We'd be talking, and in his frustration he would suddenly yell at me. It was like being caught in the path of a flamethrower. The intensity and fullness, the heat, of his sudden rage would strike me. When I was younger, it would stun me into silence. Later, it would provoke me to rage. My rage lacked the intensity and volume of his, but I think its very presence surprised him. Sometimes that's all it took—a quick return blast from me, and he would settle down again. But sometimes his rage was overflowing, and he would continue, and then I would say something like, "Fuck you, Hunter, I'm leaving. I'm not going to talk to you. You're out of control," and walk across the yard to the cabin.

I did not expect that Will's presence would change my relationship with Hunter. I also did not expect that Will's birth would bring the five of us—Hunter, Deb, Jennifer, Will, and me—together into a family. But it did. Will became the focus. When we came up to Owl Farm, there were always new toys, some that Deb had found at garage sales, and some that Hunter had ordered. As Will got a bit older, he would sit at the end of the kitchen counter and eat his lunch while Hunter ate his breakfast in his Command Chair. Or, Will would stand on the couch in front of the kitchen counter, facing Hunter over the typewriter, and Hunter would grab something and give it to Will to play with, and they would talk nonsense. When it was time for Will to go to sleep, Hunter said to put him in his bedroom, and when Will started to cry when he saw the masks and stuffed animals, wolverines or skunks or foxes, in the bedroom, Hunter said, go ahead and cover them with sheets. One night when Will was asleep on the bed, without warning Hunter retired early, and when Jen and I went looking for him, we found him and Will sleeping together on his bed, curled up on their sides. It is an image I will not forget.

When we came to visit, there was nearly always a present for Will. There might be a novelty like a plastic hammer that made a sound of breaking glass when it struck something, or a book on the history of tractors, which were a major focus for Will when he was around two years old. One time it was a little seat that could be hung from the ceiling from a springy rope. I was going to put the hook in a door frame, but Hunter insisted that the seat be hung in the middle of the kitchen, where Will could bounce and thrash his legs right alongside the Pitkin County sheriff, or the past president of the National Association of Criminal Defense Lawyers (NACDL), or one of the wild artist/carpenters who lived up the road, while everyone was watching football. Hunter wanted Will in the action. It was important that he learn at a young age the difference between an option and a lateral pass, or the folly of betting with your heart rather than your head in a big game. We drew the line, though, when Hunter insisted that Will throw down twenty dollars, the house bet, on the game.

For Christmas one year it was a small wooden rocking horse painted in bright colors, another year a miniature piano from Hammacher Schlemmer. Another time it was a block and tackle made of hardwood and painted red and blue. I rigged up an eye-bolt in a door frame, fastened a bucket to the lifting end of the block and tackle, and demonstrated to Will how it worked. He studied it carefully, and Hunter watched him watch the mechanism move.

There was also the tractor and the convertible. Hunter had bought a small John Deere farm tractor to mow the two-acre lawn at Owl Farm. It had a front-loader bucket and a huge three-blade mowing attachment that hooked to the rear. Knowing Will's fondness for tractors, Hunter started it up and took Will for a ride. He sat between Hunter's legs, not even two years old, while Hunter steered with one hand and held Will with the other, and I sat on the fender as Hunter drove over the lawn and around the house. Will smiled the whole time and could have probably ridden for hours, except Hunter couldn't do it—the jarring and lurching of the tractor was hell on his joints. Later, when Will would get bored being in the house, Deb would take his hand and they would visit the tractor, and Will would climb in the bucket or on the front tire, or dangle his tiny legs over the edge of the seat while Deb hovered by him.

· · ·

Doting Aunt Deb with Will in the
kitchen at Owl Farm, Christmas 1999

WHEN WILL WAS TWELVE and Hunter had been dead six years, I taught him to drive that tractor. I know Hunter would have been proud to see him confidently throwing the tractor in gear, engaging and disengaging the clutch, and scooping up the odd tire or block from the ground. I taught Will to shoot because of the thrill and because it is important to understand and respect guns rather than fear them, but also because I learned all about guns from my father. I have found a great comfort in passing on a family tradition or skill. It grounds me in something beyond myself and this day.

There were the presents, and there was also the bonfire. When Will was four, Hunter had a bonfire made for him during one of our visits. Unknown to us, over the previous year Deb had been planning this event, collecting dead trees, branches, and random flammable objects that littered the property into a giant pile about fifty yards behind his house. It was late winter, there was a thin layer of snow on the ground, the sky was overcast, and the ground was wet. The time had come to light the fire. Hunter led us out back to the great pile, and soon Joe, a friend and neighbor who was a volunteer fireman, drove up in an old red fire engine just in case the fire got out of hand. Joe soaked the pile in gasoline and then set the match to it. We stood out there for hours, well back from the intense heat of the fire, watching the flames leap and flicker far above our heads as the sky darkened and night fell, until it was time to go inside. The next morning Will and

Ace and Will at the kitchen counter in 2002 with the iguana we gave Hunter. He was still the doting grandfather.

I went back to the site of the fire and found it still smoldering, the coals still glowing red below the surface ash. It took another day for the fire to go out completely, and even then there were probably hot coals buried deep in the ashes. Long afterward, Deb would take Will (after they had explored the tractor) to poke through the ashes and search for treasures.

Will brought a completeness. I was no longer only a son, I was a father, with my father. I saw how he loved my son, and I understood better how my father loved me. For those weekends the five of us created a circle of protection from the chaos of the outside world, and inside that circle there was love, and acceptance, and connection, and family that I craved. I am positive that he wanted us there that last weekend for that reason, so that he could take his own life while standing in that circle with us.

It's strange and sad that that which took him away from us that weekend was also one of the threads binding us. The man loved his guns. And I loved guns because of him. They brought us together. Isn't that a perfect American story? Guns brought us together. And a gun took him away.

Guns were always around in my childhood—shotguns leaning in the corner by the hall to the bedrooms, by the doorway to the living room, and by the front door. The ammo was stacked on shelves in the kitchen. Every kind of ammo: 12 gauge in multiple shot size, 20 gauge, .410 gauge, boxes of .22 ammo, 9mm, .357, .44, .38, .223, .45, hollow points, fully jacketed, it was all there, stacked behind the glass doors of the country cabinets. Where another family would have put china and knickknacks, we had a small armory, tools, batteries, screws, and of course the ultraviolet head zapper, a thing out of the '40s that had various glass neon-filled attachments that fit into a heavy black handle. Hunter would bring this out during parties, turn down the lights, plug this thing in, and wave it around as a purple glow emanated from the glass and it buzzed ominously.

Guns had made it hard between us too. I have never forgotten that incident with his fancy pellet gun when I was twelve, his hard anger, my shame, my anger too, at this bastard grinding me down, forcing me to carry that little metal sight to remind me of how I had fucked up. I still haven't quite forgiven him for that, though it's so long ago now I wonder why it matters to me still.

I remember sitting in the kitchen on the couch, Hunter in the Command Chair at the kitchen counter behind me, a shotgun barrel across my lap, the gun cleaning supplies spread out around me. Some basketball or football game was always on the TV, or maybe CNN. There was the rustle of Hunter's newspaper, either the news or the sports section, and the acrid smell of cigarette smoke, always the cigarette smoke. I used to hate it, but after many years of going to visit Hunter, it stopped bothering me. It was a part of him, like the whiskey and beer and late nights, and in a strange way it was reassuring.

The smell of Hoppe's gun solvent was another comforting smell; it connected me with my father. I was in no hurry, not paying attention to the time, just cleaning the gun. I'd take a cotton square, saturate it with solvent, put it on the tip of the cleaning rod, and push it into the barrel. At first the cotton square would come out dark gray, even black, coated with gunpowder residue. I'd hold up the filthy square to Hunter, he would look up at it, grunt with approval, and resume reading. I would drop the square on the floor along with other used cotton squares and take a new square, saturate it, and push it through the barrel. With each pass the square came out a bit cleaner, from black to dark gray to light gray to just touched with gray. I'd hold up this last swab for Hunter's inspection, and he would grunt again. A grunt was good.

Once the swabs came out clean, I'd hold up the barrel, point it at a light source, and look through it just to make sure I hadn't missed anything. Any stray grains of powder would show up as tiny black specks against the silver smooth interior of the barrel. When the interior of the barrel was flawless, I'd put a bit of gun oil on a swab and run that through the barrel to prevent rust. I'd then set it aside and start work on the rest of the gun, cleaning around the firing pins, the pivots where the barrel joined with the stock and trigger mechanism, until those swabs were pure white also. When this was done, I'd put a bit of gun oil on a cloth and run that over all the metal parts of the gun as a protective covering.

Finally, I'd reattach the barrel to the rest of the gun and close it with a clean snap, a smooth, slightly oil-dampened snap of two precisely milled parts coming together perfectly with no extra play, no jiggling, no resistance, just a perfect fit. I would pass it to Hunter, holding it with a cloth to avoid touching the barrel. He would take the gun, tilt his head back a bit so he could look through his reading glasses, and examine it. At first he would carefully look it over, but later this became an act, his part in the ritual. He would grunt, or nod, or say, "good," then hand it back to me. I would carry the gun back to the gun safe, carefully slide it back into the cushioned rack alongside the others, and select the next for cleaning. I don't know how long each gun took. Maybe twenty minutes, maybe an hour, but it didn't matter. I wasn't in any hurry.

People told me how proud he was of me, and I wonder if he was proud of me, in part, for playing my role in our ritual. For another father it might have been working on a car, or tying flies, or gutting a deer, some task that needed to be done that had been passed on and therefore was a shared experience. Those nights, and there were many of them over the years, are precious to me, and I hope were precious to him also.

The night before he died he asked me if I wanted the guns when he was gone. I said, of course. He said, "You're going to shoot them, right?" I said, of course. It went without saying that I would clean them too, carefully and thoroughly.

Each time we came to visit there came a point in the evening (because it was always evening when we came, and evening when we left) when I would ask him which guns needed cleaning, or he would say, "The .45 needs cleaning. It's filthy," or whichever gun he had been shooting recently. I'd ask, "Is it in the safe?" Usually it was, but sometimes it would be closer to hand. He always kept a pistol in a cabinet next to his Command Chair, hidden from view but easy to grab if he needed it. And unlike every other gun in the house, this one was loaded. Sometimes he would reach down, grab that gun—it might be the compact Walther PPK, made famous by James Bond, or maybe the .45, always a semiauto, though, not a revolver—and hand it to me over the counter. I would take it carefully, as if there were nothing unusual about a man having a gun next to his office chair in the kitchen, pop the magazine out, make sure the breech was clear of shells, set it down, and get the gun cleaning tool kit from the closet next to the gun safe in my old bedroom. Pistols, especially semiauto pistols, were hard to clean.

Some pistols could be disassembled for cleaning, like the World War I German Luger. It was like a 3-D puzzle: swivel this lever, pull it this way, pull the slide, push the barrel, and suddenly it came apart. I remember Hunter pointing out that each part in a Luger was stamped with the corresponding number, so that when German officers were cleaning their guns, there was no chance of mixing up parts. I never tried to take that gun apart by myself—what if I broke it? I would take it to Hunter and let him break it down for me. I cleaned the parts and gave them back. He reassembled it, and I put it away in the gun safe.

That night before he died, he took the .45 semiauto pistol from its place in the cabinet by his chair and handed it to me. It was no big deal, just another gun that needed cleaning. I ejected the magazine and checked the breech like I always did, cleaned the barrel, and put a thin coat of oil over everything so that the action slid smoothly and it glistened in the light. It was not one of the prettier guns he owned, but it was well suited to stopping people if that's what was necessary, and given Hunter's diverse and sometimes crazy fan base, not to mention enraged boyfriends or husbands of women over the years, there was no telling who might show up with a gun, ready to avenge some wrong. And every now and then they did.

Hunter examining a pistol I have just cleaned
in the kitchen at Owl Farm, 2003

It was that same gun, the .45 semiauto, that he used to shoot himself the day after I cleaned it. He took it from me, cleaned, polished, and oiled, in perfect working order, knowing he would shoot himself in the head that weekend. I haven't seen that gun since. It was confiscated by the sheriff as evidence that day.

Years later, Hunter's lawyer returned the unfired bullets from that gun to me. I have them in a Ziploc bag pinned to the wall in front of my desk. On the shell around the primer is stamped, FEDERAL .45 AUTO. The slug is copper-coated, fully jacketed. If I examined them carefully, I would find my father's fingerprints on them. I have not touched them and do not plan to.

Like swimming and cleaning the guns, tending the fire was another ritual. If we arrived in fall or winter, my first job was either to start a fire, or tend to the fire, just as it had been when I was a child. It was a point of pride for me to avoid the fire-starting shortcuts like starter sticks or fire logs that Hunter had given in to in the intervening years, and to build the fire as he had taught me. It was important that I do this because it was part of our ritual. When I came home, I was the fire tender.

Jennifer and I usually brought something for Hunter each time we visited. It might be a gag gift or something small: chocolate truffles, music, hot sauce, a book. At Christmas the gifts were more elaborate. Up until Will was born, Jen and I would make him a gift each year. One year it was a Jacob's ladder, a high-voltage transformer attached to two metal poles, between which an electric arc would travel slowly upward until it reached the top and vanished, to be replaced by a new arc at the base (think of the lab in an old Frankenstein movie). If you put a piece of paper in the path of the arc, it would burn dozens of tiny holes in the paper as it passed over it. Deborah said that at parties, Hunter would bring it from the living room, set it on the kitchen counter, and light his cigarette with it, his face a couple of inches from a ten-thousand-volt arc. It was dramatic and impressive to his audience. She said that he would then announce with pride, "My son made it for me."

Another year we made him a mobile out of old radio tubes and bullets. A third year we fitted an old black rotary phone with TV tubes, buttons, and dials we had found at an electronics flea market. Another year we decorated a dartboard with Christmas lights, a picture of Nixon on one side and the Dalai Lama on the other, and various random things hanging from it. He hung that proudly in the window, so everyone would see it as they arrived.

In turn, on each visit, as we prepared to depart, Hunter would give us things. It was always last-minute. We would have our coats on and be ready to walk out the door, and Hunter would mumble in an offhand way, as if he were embarrassed to be asking, "How are your tires?" or, "You have enough gas? Here, take this," and he would push a hundred-dollar bill into my hand. Or he would grope around for something else, whatever was close by. One time it was a travel clock, another time a miniature shortwave radio. I didn't begin to understand until after Jen's first visit to meet Hunter one New Year's Eve. As we were leaving she said to me, "Wow. Your dad is very proud of you." I was pleased, but confused. I said, "Why do you say that?" "You can tell by the way he looks at you," she said. "Why do you think he gives you all this stuff when you leave? He loves you very much." She explained that he used the gifts instead of words.

I gradually began to see what she was talking about. It was like learning a new language, except that in this case I hadn't even recognized it as a language to be decoded. In giving me a hundred dollars for gas, or buying new snow tires for our car, or giving me a travel clock, he was telling me that he loved me. On our next visit I paid attention, and when upon leaving he pressed into my hands a million-watt car spotlight, or a leather duck decoy, I imagined that he was telling me he loved me. I didn't say anything, of course, but I accepted it.

As we were walking out the back door, Hunter would say, "Call me when you get home. Let me know you made it." We would agree, and when we got home, I would call him. The check-in phone call from home was the unbinding ritual. I would say, "We made it home safely. Uneventful." He would say, "Good. Good." Then I would say, "It was a good weekend. Thanks." One time I told him, "I love you, Hunter." It was the first time I ever had said this. He mumbled and hung up. By that time, I didn't take it as a rejection. Some time later, after a good visit, as

Will holding his stuffed monkey, George, by the tail on the hill overlooking Owl Farm, spring 2002

Jen and I were getting in the car, he stood in the doorway, and as I was swinging the door open, he said, "I love you, man," then ducked inside.

Sometimes when it was time for us to go, he would be asleep. There was something wonderfully childlike about Hunter in sleep. He would be asleep on his side, with a hand under his head, his knees up slightly, in a faint suggestion of the fetal position. His face was peaceful, all the pride, anger, and humor gone. The bedroom had a faint bitter smell of his sweat, and though it was a large room it felt close and cozy, a room for sleeping, not working, thinking, or even talking. The windows were always covered by curtains or blankets, and there were bookshelves holding his favorite books on three walls. To let the unfiltered sunlight strike that room would have been wrong, it would have disrupted its insulated quality. That's what it felt like—as if the room were wrapped in an insulation that dampened everything—light, sound, thought, and even anxiety. It was his inner sanctum, and I entered it with the appropriate reverence.

I would sit down on the bed beside him and shake his arm gently and call his name, then again a bit harder and a bit louder. Eventually he would moan. I would tell him I was leaving, and he would mumble something. I realized that often he wasn't actually awake, and that he would have no recollection of my waking him. But sometimes he would be awake, and we would have a short conversation. I talked in a low voice not because there was a need but because the room required quiet. Those brief times, maybe a dozen, when I sat beside him on the bed, were some of our most intimate moments, not because of what we said, but because at those times we both were less guarded. It was as if there in the bedroom, and at the Stranahans' pool, we were protected and could set aside the armor. I think for Hunter it was the vulnerability of sleep combined with the safety of his sanctum. For me it was the privilege of being with him in his unarmored state. Eventually, I would tell him I had to go, that I loved him, and walk quietly out of the room, almost on tiptoe though it was carpeted. Once across the threshold of the bedroom door I was in the outside world again. But for those minutes in the bedroom I felt blessed.

IN THOSE LAST ten or so years we had built up enough mutual trust that I could take part in the writing process from time to time. Hunter started work on his book about the 1992 presidential campaign, *Better Than Sex*, in 1993, just after Clinton was elected to his first term, and continued for the next year or so until it was published in 1994. It is a disjointed book filled with flashes of brilliance, power, humor, and insight. Once Clinton got the Democratic nomination and it was clear he had a shot at winning, Hunter was in frequent contact with the campaign staffers, often in the form of faxes. There were hundreds of faxes between Hunter and Clinton's top campaign staff, George Stephanopoulos and James Carville. It was more like a scrapbook that consisted mostly of correspondence in the form of actual photos of the faxes. This made Hunter's job much easier: he just had to write transitions or fillers.

It was a wild, chaotic effort, and at critical moments he recruited Jennifer and me to help. It seemed like it was all happening at once—selecting the faxes, deciding on the organization of the book, writing chapter subheads, and researching facts. But the real problem was that Hunter couldn't focus on writing. He would find a million ways to put it off. There were football games to watch, and if not football, then basketball. There was the news. Or maybe he had stayed up two nights in a row and was so exhausted that there was no question of useful work that night. There were people coming over most every afternoon and evening to say hello, watch a game, talk politics. There were long phone calls. There were always drugs.

Pot was always sure to mellow him, make him smile, and laugh, and cause him to lose his train of thought. It was when he had had a few hits of pot or hash that he loved to tell stories. He would sit on his stool, rocking back and forth slightly, grinning often as he remembered something, or laughing at his own story. The stories would usually start in one place and wander, branch, and diverge until an hour later you had long forgotten the initial episode, but it didn't matter because he was such a captivating storyteller. Other drugs, like acid, brought out a sharper side, sometimes playful, but sometimes cruel. An hour or so after he took LSD, his mood would turn, and it was time for us to say good night and go to the cabin. Cocaine and booze didn't even qualify as drugs, they were a staple of his daily diet, like pink grapefruit, orange juice, and vitamins.

There was always anxiety or depression to distract him—maybe the money situation was getting critical, or a legal problem was making him edgy. Or maybe he just felt so depressed he didn't feel like writing anything. As a last resort he could always pick a fight with someone—his girlfriend, the writing assistant of the day, or Deb were the most likely targets. Eventually a combination of shame and fear finally drove him to the typewriter late at night. The next morning there might be a page, but sometimes there were only a few sentences.

It was hard to watch. I felt terrible for him. Hunter was a perfectionist, and he was a damn fine writer, and I know it killed him to realize he wasn't going to write anything, hit the power switch on the IBM Selectric typewriter, and retreat to the bedroom, leaving an empty page.

Other times, though, when there was movement and energy, it was a wonderful thing to be a part of. I remember sitting at the end of the counter reading parts of the book and then discussing it. This was tricky. On one hand, Hunter wanted honest feedback, including the negative. But he wasn't always gracious about receiving it, and as for giving advice on what he should write, that was pointless. I kept my comments to a minimum, focusing on what I liked and not commenting on what didn't work.

I didn't realize until much later, after his death, that what he needed from those around him wasn't advice on how to fix what was broken, but encouragement. He needed us to tell him that he *could* write, that he was a brilliant writer, that he just had to keep going, that this line was funny, or that line was really well written. He needed cheerleaders. With that encouragement, he would get excited, would turn the TV down, roll a new piece of paper in, and start to type. He would start to throw ideas out and if they were well received he would throw more ideas out. He would go quiet for several minutes while he typed, and then the back-and-forth of ideas and encouragement would resume. His eyes would brighten and he would sit up straight at the typewriter.

Those were the best times, when Hunter remembered for a little while what a fine writer he was by actually doing it. He loved the praise and literary recognition that had come to him in the last ten or fifteen years of his life, but ultimately he needed to feel the words flowing through him onto the page and see their effect on an audience. Those long stretches without sleep were really hard on me, but it was well worth it to be a part of Hunter's writing life, especially seeing my father having fun writing, doing what he was born to do, and doing it well.

But the fact was that he no longer had the ability to complete a book-length project. *Better Than Sex* was the last book that contained new writing. After this point, every book was a collection of previously written or published material. Three years later the first letters book, *The Proud Highway,* was published. The year after that, in 1998, *The Rum Diary,* his only novel, was published, some thirty-eight years after it was written and rejected by numerous publishers. In 2000, the second letters book, *Fear and Loathing in America,* was published, followed by *Kingdom of Fear* in 2003 and the last book, *Hey Rube,* in 2004. These books consisted entirely of writing he had already done—as a young man in Puerto Rico or his correspondence over the years, his ESPN columns, or various previously unpublished work. Even completing the weekly ESPN column became an epic adventure, or maybe a nightmare. A thousand words were all he could manage, and that under extreme duress. His powers of observation had not decreased, and in those short bursts you could often see his native brilliance and hear the powerful music of his voice in the words, but he couldn't sustain it.

A couple years after *Better Than Sex* was published, Jen and I helped Hunter with the first book of letters, *The Proud Highway.* Douglas Brinkley, the presidential historian and author who by this time had become a close friend of Hunter's, suggested it as a way to publish a book without actually having to write one. It was a painful but realistic assessment: Hunter needed money, the only way to bring in money was to write another book, but that was a very, very long shot. A book of letters was a great solution:

the letters were very good, something Hunter could be proud of, and it was a book that could be put together with very little work on Hunter's part.

When Jen and I came to visit Owl Farm, we were put to work in the War Room looking for material. Though Hunter had not used it for writing in around twenty years, it was still the place where the most important or sensitive papers, tapes, and videos were kept. Over the years, I had gone in at Hunter's request to find something in particular, but never casually. The War Room and Hunter's bedroom were both off-limits to everyone besides Deb, even to me, unless I had his permission. For Hunter to permit Jennifer and me to work in the War Room and go through his papers while he remained upstairs was a gigantic show of trust in us. Also, Hunter had a pretty good idea of what we would find as we went through the papers.

Hunter was a pack rat. The only things that left that house were the trash bags from the kitchen or gifts. Everything else was stored in the basement or the barn. At one point I went looking for the bicycle that I received on my eighth birthday. I hadn't seen it in thirty years. I found it in the loft in the barn, no longer shiny but still serviceable. I pumped up the tires, tightened a few bolts, and my son was riding it ten minutes later. I found my stuffed animals from when I was ten. The closets downstairs were full of Hunter's clothes from forty years ago—one year when I was in college I asked him if I could have two sport coats that were bought in a men's shop in Louisville, Kentucky, probably in the early '60s. He agreed to lend them to me. He had boxes of *Playboy* magazines, going back to the '70s. He had generations of luggage, a marijuana distiller he had been given as a gift, a speargun, a crossbow, boxes of ammunition, posters in mailing tubes, old wooden doors painted in the '60s in psychedelic colors, a barred door from a bank vault—and papers, boxes and boxes and boxes of his papers, what we began to call The Archive.

Our job was to go through every single box in the War Room, extract letters, and file them by year. Some boxes were filled with thoroughly nibbled newspapers and thousands of mouse droppings, some had photos, some various drafts of books or articles, some had objects—one box contained a few hundred bars of hotel-size, yellowing, now-withered Neutrogena soap, another hundreds of matchbooks that Hunter had collected from around the country in his decades of traveling. It was a cornucopia, a potpourri, a random history of Hunter's life from the age of seventeen to the present. There was no order to the boxes, and few were labeled, so we grabbed the nearest box and began sifting.

Part of the job included using our judgment to exclude letters deemed too personal: for example, letters between Sandy and Hunter. He was very concerned that Sandy might object to these being published, and asked her permission before including letters to her in the book. That meant we had to read them. I knew it was significant that he trusted Doug, Deb, Jennifer, and me enough to let us go through these papers, but as I reflect on it now, I understand more completely the magnitude of his decision. He knew what was in those boxes. Not all of it was flattering. Hunter, a man who was intensely private about his personal affairs, was opening his thoroughly documented life to us, knowing we would come across letters or items that revealed some of his darker aspects. I can see now that he had come to believe that I would love him regardless of what we found.

Jen was able to move at a good pace, but for me it was a sud-

den and deep immersion in nostalgia. I found pictures from
my childhood at Owl Farm, our dogs, birthday parties, Hunter
and Sandy sitting on the couch, smiling. I found report cards
and assessments from my fourth-grade teachers, a declaration of
independence I wrote to my parents after an unjust imprison-
ment in my room when I was eight, a steno notebook of Hunter's
from a trip to Idaho in 1964, a pair of dusty, scratched yellow
Ray-Ban sunglasses. While Jen would identify a letter by reading
the first few lines and then set it aside for filing, I would read the
entire letter along with the other side of the conversation, often
stapled or paper-clipped to Hunter's letter. I was absorbing my
father in tiny increments. And it had to have been very difficult

Jen, Will, and me, in front of the bonfire while fireman Joe
Fredericks stands by. Deb had piled up all kinds of scrap lumber
from around the property to create a bonfire for Will, 2002.

for Hunter. He acknowledges in the introduction to *The Proud Highway* that it was a profoundly uncomfortable process to have other people, even family and as close a friend as Doug Brinkley, going through the letters of one's youth. While we worked, Hunter sat on his stool in the kitchen, reading the paper, watching the news, hyperaware of the activity below him while trying to ignore it. He didn't want us to discuss the letters—that would come later, after Doug had selected the best ones and needed contextual information for them, but every now and then if someone found an especially good letter, we would bring it upstairs and read it out loud.

I wasn't much help those nights, since I couldn't skim over letters between Hunter and my mother, Hunter and his brothers, Hunter and his mother. I found one letter in which Hunter explained to my mother that if she really wanted to get married, that was fine, but he wasn't going to change his ways, and that she needed to understand that going in. And he did not change his ways. I'm pretty sure that there were plenty of women in Hunter's life the whole time he was married to my mother. Does the fact that he warned her up front let him off the hook? Hell if I know. It didn't stop my mother from being very hurt and angry when she found evidence of one of those relationships on his credit-card statements when I was twelve, and telling me what a bastard he was for cheating on her.

I found another letter from my mother to Hunter, berating him for yelling at me for playing with his records when I was three or four years old. I had never known that my mother had stood up to him on my behalf and risked his rage.

I also found some of the letters that made their way into the book, the letters to friends arguing about politics and philosophy, or the letters to creditors pretending to be crazy, or the provocative letters to prospective employers explaining just what he would and would not do, take him or leave him.

Hunter gradually lost the ability to sustain the necessary concentration to write, almost certainly because of the cocaine and booze. He wasn't a binge cokehead. Hunter snorted a little bit all day, probably to balance the whiskey, but I'm sure it impaired his ability to concentrate. Then, just as he was a maintenance cocaine user, he was also a maintenance drinker, not a binger. But a fifth of whiskey a day for forty years takes its toll on the body, no matter how strong the constitution. In the last ten or so years of his life, Hunter was often sick with a variety of ailments, sometimes the usual cold or flu, but also things like fungal growths, throat infections, nasal infections, cuts and bruises, and occasional seizures. The cuts and bruises were not a result of drunken stumbling, but instead a result of his decreasing ability to walk unassisted. First the degeneration of his hip joint, then of his lower back, caused him such pain that he avoided walking as much as possible, and when he did have to walk, he would prop himself up on counters, chairs, bookcases, anything that could provide him extra support. Every now and then he missed, or slipped, and ended up cutting or bruising himself. There would be a lot of roaring and yelling, blood and excitement (he had a tremendously high pain threshold, but a very low screaming threshold) while the wound was tended to, and then he would settle down. The problem was not the bruise or the cut, but the fact that they took so long to heal. His immune system had been so beaten down that a cut that used to heal in a few days could now take weeks.

There was also the effect of long-term alcoholism on his muscles, something called alcoholic neuropathy, in which the nerves are actually poisoned by the alcohol. Gradually his muscles lost their ability to work properly, and this showed up in his walking, and as incontinence.

Toward the end, in the last year, I remember him standing in the kitchen one afternoon in his bathrobe, and he suddenly cursed and grabbed the bottom of his robe and pulled it up between his legs like a diaper. He didn't say what had happened, and I pretended I hadn't seen it and left the room so he could deal with it privately.

I didn't want to see that my father's body was falling apart, that he was not in control of himself. He was Hunter, powerful and confident, sometimes frightening, always in control of the

Hunter with Deb, the woman who knew
him and loved him best, in 2003

situation. Though he was first and always a writer, he was also an athlete, in the sense that he was firmly rooted in his body and its power. It was his trusted accomplice in every adventure and it gave him great pleasure in myriad ways throughout his life. His favorite photos were those in which he stood bare-chested, throwing a football, or piloting his boat through the Florida Keys, or wearing nothing but a pistol in a shoulder holster with a red leather jacket like some pornographic version of James Bond.

From his writing he seems to have had an affinity for certain aspects of Buddhism, but one of the central pillars of Buddhism—acceptance—was not one of them. On the contrary, he was a life-long advocate and practitioner of changing his reality to suit his wishes. Hunter was not one to accept the gradual deterioration of his body. He endured it as long as he could, and then when it was no longer endurable, and he understood it was only going to get worse, he checked out.

NINE

THE LAST DAY

I HAD LAST VISITED my father in late November 2004, just before Jennifer and Will and I went to Europe for a month. I went up alone to see him for a few days.

Hunter was preparing for a trip to New Orleans that he was excited about, though he was still recovering from a broken leg.

All I remember from that visit was watching *The Big Sleep* together, just the two of us alone at Owl Farm. We savored the impeccable dialogue, the cinematography, the acting.

Jen, Will, and I returned from England and Italy right about New Year's Day. Because we had missed Christmas and New Year's with Hunter, we were determined to see him soon. We had planned to go up in January, but in all the turmoil of our return, we had to reschedule for mid-February.

We arrived on a Friday night. It was late afternoon when we drove up the Roaring Fork Valley and a storm was moving through. As we passed Carbondale I pulled over a few times to take photos of the wispy clouds that were clinging to the hills along the highway, and to admire Mount Sopris, partially shrouded in cloud. When we got to Owl Farm I took more photos. The light was beautiful, the soft gray of a cloudy late-winter afternoon infused with a glow from the sun coming through the patches of blue sky. I took photos of the sunset and then of Owl Farm, which looked warm and safe with its windows glowing in the winter twilight.

On Saturday afternoon Will, who was six at the time, was eating his lunch at the end of the counter in the kitchen while Hunter sat on his stool. Hunter asked Will what he was studying in school. Will said he was studying mysteries. He said that a forensic scientist had come into his school the week before to explain what he did. Will asked Hunter, "Do you know what the difference between murder and suicide is?" Hunter said, "What?" Will said, "Suicide is self-kill." Hunter said, "That is exactly right." Will went on to explain how a forensic investigator could tell if a death by gunshot was a murder or a suicide based on the trajectory of the bullet. Then they had a conversation about Sherlock Holmes.

Saturday night started off well. Hunter insisted we watch a movie, *The Maltese Falcon,* one of his favorites. It was a quiet, peaceful time that bound Will, Jen, Hunter, and me together even though we weren't having a conversation. He was calm and present. I sat in the chair at the end of the counter, Anita was in the wingback Hunter had stolen from a Ralph Lauren store, and Jen and Will were on the couch. The movie ended and there was contentment in the air. Good movies gave Hunter a respite from his worries, some baseless and others well founded, which haunted him most of the time. He was feeling playful and he pulled a pellet gun from a cabinet under the counter where he sat. He aimed across the room and through the living room doorway at a large Tibetan gong that he had received as a Christmas gift several years earlier. The path of the pellet was unnervingly close to Anita's head where she sat, and unnerving her was the point. He was showing off his marksmanship, but that was never sufficient with Hunter. There had to be an element of unpredictability, of the potential for injury, arrest, and a scene for Hunter to be really satisfied. I experienced it countless times, and never got used to it. Hunter needed a straight man for his act, and tonight it was Anita. She protested but that only encouraged Hunter, and he squeezed off a round that passed in front of Anita and struck the gong squarely. Anita lost her temper, stood in front of him and began yelling, accusing him of recklessness, stupidity, and cruelty. She threatened to call the police, to have his guns taken away, and to have him put in a nursing home. She announced that she'd be sleeping in the guest room downstairs.

He and I began to talk. It was sometime that night when Hunter told me that he wanted me to have certain items when he died. He pointed to the silver medallion from Oscar that was hanging on the lamp on the kitchen counter, then to the old clock from his mother, the silver julep cups, then to the silver filigreed box from his grandmother. Then he asked me to take them with me when I left for Denver the next day, everything except for the medallion. I said, half joking, "Is there something I should know?" He mumbled or didn't respond. I packed the cups, the filigreed box, and the clock into our basket of things.

Looking back, it seems so obvious that he was planning to kill himself imminently. These items were some of his most treasured, and he had not only been telling me that he wanted me to have them when he died, but he gave them to me that night. But there was no other way. When I asked him if there was something I should know, he could not have answered me truthfully. It would have created an impossible dilemma for us both.

This is a difficult truth for me to accept even now. I have told people that my only regret was that I didn't ask him more questions, but the fact is that wasn't the basis of our relationship. He didn't want me to ask him questions about his childhood, about his greatest regret, his truest love, why his marriage to Sandy had failed, how he felt about his writing, his mother, his friends, Woody Creek, or sex. I wish I knew the answers to these questions, but that would not have created intimacy between us. It would have been an interview, it would have been probing for his soul, for the "real" Hunter S. Thompson. There was far more connection that November night a few months earlier when he and I watched *The Big Sleep*. It was something we shared together. There was no self-consciousness, no awkward and presumptuous soul probing, just our shared enthusiasm for a great movie.

I used to enjoy talking about politics with him because it was a topic we both cared very much about, and I knew enough to have an informed opinion. But the intimacy was not in the information we shared or in the opinions he expressed, and it wasn't in any novel or contrary opinions of my own that I shared with him. I wanted to impress him with my knowledge and insight, but now I understand that all that really mattered was that we were talking together. We could have been talking about sheep farming or geologic timescales or plant fertilizer. Politics was a topic that we could talk about, but it wasn't the content of the words, it was the act of having a conversation that connected us.

I could have regrets that we didn't talk more, that I didn't take his calls at three a.m. because I was just too damn tired. Had I answered the phone, though, I would have dreaded and then resented his calls and his rambling talk when I had to get up in two hours for work, knowing I would be exhausted for the next two days. Not taking these calls was an arrangement that worked for us.

In the same way, I avoided getting caught up in the endless dramas of his life. When I was younger, I would take these dramas seriously, worry about them, and try to fix them. I would offer solutions, but he didn't want solutions. We would both get frustrated, I would give up, the particular drama would unfold or evaporate, and his life would go on its wild, bumpy, adrenaline-filled, dramatic course that he evidently preferred. I learned to keep a certain distance from the daily madness of his life.

That Sunday morning the three of us, Hunter, Jen, and I, stayed up for a while longer, and then Jen and I took Will next door to the guest cabin. It was time for Jen and Will to go to sleep for the night. I tucked them in, and Jennifer told me several times to pay attention. She said it was very important that I pay close attention to everything Hunter said and did that night. I replied that I would, not really understanding, but trusting her instincts. I returned to the house and talked with Hunter for another couple of hours.

By six a.m. I could no longer stay awake. I had been up almost twenty-four hours and I couldn't focus. I was at the ragged end, and though he would sometimes offer me drugs to stay awake, in that way that gentlemen do when lighting up a cigarette in the presence of another, I always refused.

This was a line I would not cross. In the last few years I would have a beer with him while watching a football game, or late at night have a "biff," a 2-1 mix of Chivas and Baileys Irish Cream, but that was the extent of my drinking with Hunter. I may have once had a hit off of a joint with him, but I was never a fan of marijuana because it made me stupid, and I wanted to be at my sharpest with my father. He had no patience for stupid people, even when they were female, young, and sexy. LSD was out as well. I had been a fan of acid in my youth, and I know it was perhaps Hunter's favorite drug, but he never offered it, and I would not have taken it, certainly not with him. LSD is not a casual drug. It is a ceremonial drug. And I believe Hunter thought of it the same way. He called it "Walking with the King."

I think Hunter preferred his family and lovers to be relatively drug-free. I think he was relieved each time I turned down the offered pipe or powder. I also think he considered the fact that I was not a drunk or drug fiend was a vindication of his parenting. That I emerged from that maelstrom of his own life appearing relatively normal filled him with wonder and pride.

That Sunday was a lovely winter day. The snow was deep and dazzling, the sky a pure blue. Jennifer and Will took advantage of the day to go sledding. The driveway up to our friend Ed Bastian's house on the mesa was perfectly suited for sledding with several inches of new snow, slightly melted by the sun and southern exposure. They went up and down the driveway while I sat at the end of the counter with Hunter.

Around three p.m., Jen and Will came back inside, flushed and happy. Hunter and I took a break. Jennifer and Will got into the hot tub in the back room to warm up, then moved to the living room couch to play 20 Questions. Hunter was reading the paper and watching TV, I was taking pictures of a Gonzo mosaic that Jennifer had made for Hunter the previous year. It was just the three of us and Hunter, quiet and intimate, the four of us sharing the insular and warm peace of the house. I took the mosaic into the office to try to get some consistent light for the photograph. I heard a weird cry and a crack. I thought nothing of it. Hunter was famous for his peculiar vocalizations, and the thump was probably a book he had dropped or thrown.

I took the picture of the mosaic and walked out of the office to return it to its place in the living room. I looked over at Hunter in his chair and saw that his head was slumped forward on his chest. My first thought was that he had fallen asleep. I said his name. I became afraid, thinking perhaps he had had a seizure. In the last five years he had been suffering from them, a fairly common symptom of long-term alcoholism. I walked over to him, the mosaic still in my hand.

I don't know exactly what I saw that told me he was dead. There was no blood except for a tiny trickle from his mouth.

I felt suddenly cold and began to tremble. I ran into the living room to get Jennifer. As I ran I thought something like, It has finally happened. I have expected and dreaded this day for years, and now it has happened. I babbled something to Jennifer. She came running with me; Will stayed on the couch. It wasn't until weeks later that he told us that he had no idea what was happening. All he knew is that he had never seen his parents so scared.

We had to call the sheriff, Bob Braudis. We never considered calling 911. Hunter had put a sign on the refrigerator that had been there for years, "Do not call 911. This means you!" I grabbed the Rolodex and tried to find Braudis's card, but I was trembling and I could barely focus. Together we found his card. Jennifer called his mobile phone.

We had brought Hunter gifts that weekend, including a reddish-orange, almost gold, silk scarf from Florence, Italy. I put it around his neck. It seemed important. I touched his head, and it was warm, but not hot as he normally was. His body was cooling. I held his head and cried out, then I kissed his head, and went back into the living room.

I suddenly had the notion that I had to mark this moment, this tectonic shift in our lives. I grabbed the nickel-plated 12-gauge shotgun from its corner in the kitchen, loaded it with as many shells as it would hold, and walked out onto the front porch. I pointed it in the air and shot each shell, one after the other. It was a salute to my father. I hadn't planned this; it just seemed like the right thing to do. As I stood on the porch, I saw a sheriff's deputy drive by on the road in front of the house. He turned his car around and pulled into the driveway. I took the shotgun back inside and set it down. The deputy came to the door. I assumed he had already gotten the call about Hunter, but maybe not. Maybe the shotgun blasts had gotten his attention instead. I told him what happened, and he came inside. He said, "I'd like to see the shotgun." I pointed to where it was lying in the living room. I remember thinking, Does he think I shot Hunter?

I vaguely remember calling Anita on her cell phone and telling her that Hunter was dead. She cried out and began sobbing.

I remember looking at him sitting in the chair. I saw the .45 on the floor. It was in a pool of blood. What little blood there was had run down from his mouth, down his arm, and pooled on the floor right below his fingers. I remember how thick the blood looked, and how it seemed to have something else in it, some kind of clear or whitish fluid. I only looked at that pool for a second, but I will never forget it. Not ever.

Later I saw one of the deputies cleaning up the blood, and it occurred to me that there are so many mundane tasks after a death, things like cleaning up the blood, and laying the body out straight before it stiffens. I looked for a bullet hole above the stove. There was a deep crease in the metal hood over the stove where the bullet must have struck.

Then there were many people in the house. Deputies, Bob Braudis, the coroner. They laid Hunter on his back on the kitchen floor. At some point they put him into a long black plastic body bag and zipped it up. A grief counselor arrived and talked to Jennifer, Will, and me for a while. Braudis bear-hugged me and I felt like a boy.

At one point I remember standing around his body in the kitchen with the deputies and the sheriff. I poured biffs for all of us, and we toasted Hunter. Again, it seemed like the right thing to do.

It's hard to describe how strange it was to see, three hours later, a news ticker scrolling across the bottom of CNN that read "Hunter S. Thompson has just died of a self-inflicted gunshot wound" as we stood next to his body on the kitchen floor in the bag. Now things became truly surreal. Two deputies blocked the driveway with their cars and stayed all night to keep people out. They stayed for several days.

Eventually the deputies loaded his body into the back of a Suburban. I found a boom box, one of his compilation CDs, "Where were you when the fun stopped?," started the music, and placed the boom box in the back of the Suburban by Hunter's body. The driver took him to Grand Junction, a two-hour drive from Woody Creek, for the autopsy, and he played the CD over and over all the way there.

By the next day, the news trucks were parked at the driveway entrance, their satellite antennas raised to the sky. Over the next few weeks, hundreds of letters poured in, most from people I did not know, expressing sympathy, and how Hunter's life and writings had affected their lives.

I thought many times about the lack of blood and how peaceful he looked. His eyes were closed, he looked asleep except for the trickle of blood from his lips. When people heard that he shot himself in the head they assumed it was horribly bloody, like something you might see in the movies, or like Hemingway with the shotgun. But no, it was surgical, precise. I think about how much time he must have spent over the years planning exactly how he would kill himself. He had worked out what kind of gun, what kind of bullet, and where exactly to aim it so that there was no chance of surviving, and yet also so there would be minimal blood. The deputies recovered the slug. I still haven't seen it. I imagine it's in an evidence locker somewhere in the Pitkin County Sheriff's Office.

A CLOUD OF GRIEF descended. I have scattered memories of scenes, incidents, but I don't remember times. Was it a day, a week, or a month? I don't remember. I saw many people, but I don't remember who. I remember the sanctuary of the cabin where Jennifer, Will, and I could be alone. I remember a children's grief therapist in Aspen, I remember sitting around the big round table in the living room with some of Hunter's old friends trying to plan the memorial. I remember Jennifer and me being interviewed in the cabin by the *Rocky Mountain News,* and how carefully we chose our words. Jennifer took care of me: she bought me some clothes since we had only planned on a short weekend, she answered the phone, made sure I ate, kept the reporters away, and made sure the cabin was a sanctuary for the three of us.

That first week there was so much to deal with, so many decisions to make, and somehow we made them. Then everything
became cloudy. I took a month off of work, slept a lot, took long
baths, wandered around in a stupor. I returned to work, but I
can't remember much at all. I was barely functioning, and only
after nine months was my brain mostly back to normal. I didn't
need concentration or memory, though, to help plan the funeral.
It had to be both spectacular and true.

TEN

THE FUNERAL

To HIS CLOSEST FRIENDS, to his brother Davison, to Deb, to me, and to his grandson, Hunter was a man, and it was the death of that man we loved that we grieved because we would not have his presence again.

To others who knew him through his writing or through stories about him, he was a symbol, a physical manifestation of a spirit of rebellion. He made excessive drug use a part of his public persona. He expressed a ferocious idealism and a willingness to make his point using hyperbole and vicious satire. He was a literary freedom fighter who inspired either admiration or rage depending on your allegiance and perspective. He either was Jesus in the temple, raging at the money changers, or he was the devil himself.

He was also the truth teller, the shaman, the witch doctor, the outsider whose bizarre and unconventional behavior was tolerated because of his role in the tribe as the intermediary between our world and the realm of the gods who would give to us, through him, wisdom, special powers, benedictions, warnings, or curses.

In Aspen he was the fierce elder warrior chieftain to whom the community looked to enforce justice. The Lisl Auman case, in which a young woman was wrongfully sentenced to life in prison because a crazy acquaintance shot and killed a Denver police officer, is a perfect example. An injustice was brought to his attention. The more he looked into it, the clearer it became. At some point he took it on as his cause, he rallied his warriors, in this case lawyers, journalists, and celebrities. After a long, difficult campaign that eventually went to the Colorado Supreme Court, his warriors were victorious, Lisl Auman's conviction was overturned, and she was freed. Was he solely responsible? Of course not. There were many people who each did their part to ensure the victory, but without his leadership and inspiration, his determination to see justice done, and his ability to persuade others to see the importance of the cause, it wouldn't have happened.

For these reasons, this could not be an ordinary memorial. It had to be a tribute worthy of a fallen warrior. The Greeks built burial mounds, and wept and moaned and offered sacrifices to the gods when a hero died. Hunter's ceremony had to be worthy of the man.

On the third day after my father's suicide, I sat down with some of his good friends and tried to figure out how to accomplish this. We decided to hold a private commemoration on March 3, 2005, two weeks after his death, at the Hotel Jerome in downtown Aspen, a favorite place of Hunter's in the old days. The commemoration consisted of essentially a party with music, photos, and videos interspersed with testimonials from friends and family. Around four hundred people showed up. That was good and necessary. For some, it was sufficient. But it wasn't what Hunter had asked for.

He had made it very clear to me and others over the years

that when he died, he wanted to be cremated, and have his ashes shot out of a cannon at Owl Farm. He had first mentioned it back in the '70s, on a cross-country trip from Denver to Los Angeles by way of Las Vegas with his good friend and collaborator Ralph Steadman. In L.A., they stopped by a mortuary and Ralph laid out his sketch for the funeral director showing just what Hunter had in mind. This was captured in the 1978 BBC documentary *Fear and Loathing in Gonzovision*. At the end of that documentary, standing in the yard at Owl Farm, Hunter points to the bluff behind the house where he envisions the cannon standing. The drawing shows a massive tube like a mortar surmounted by a fist clutching a peyote button (a small, flat, and round light green cactus without spines, which causes hallucinations when ingested). In the documentary Hunter grabs the pen from Ralph's hand and quickly draws a second thumb on the first, telling him, "Two thumbs, Ralph. Two thumbs."

Over the years, he brought it up now and then, sometimes seemingly in jest, but often in a matter-of-fact way. That Friday night before he died, he brought it up again. Therefore, there was no question of how to proceed. A cannon would be built.

JENNIFER, A METALWORKING FRIEND of ours named John Doherty, and I discussed the options. We figured we could probably build a cannon twelve feet tall or so from steel, and we could place it up on the bluff. To make it from ordinary carbon steel would cost only a couple of hundred dollars. We considered using stainless steel instead, but that would have cost at least $10,000, maybe more, and we didn't have that kind of money. We figured we could drive it most of the way to the top of the bluff, and perhaps drag it in a sled the rest of the way. We hadn't figured out how to shoot out his ashes, but we were taking it one step at a time.

A few days later, Doug Brinkley, Hunter's good friend and editor of his letters books, came to our cabin and told us that Johnny Depp had called him and said he wanted to pay for the construction of the cannon. We were astonished. Hunter and Johnny were good friends, ever since Johnny starred in *Fear and Loathing and Las Vegas* and had shadowed Hunter for months to study his every mannerism. But it is one thing to be a friend; it is another to volunteer to build a friend's death cannon. Johnny had asked Doug to find out if that was okay with me. Johnny didn't want to do anything without my full agreement and involvement. I said yes.

Johnny came to the first commemoration on March 3. He had a suite at the Hotel Jerome. One of his assistants found me in the crowd and asked me to come with him to Johnny's room. We walked through the sitting room to the bedroom door, which was closed. I could hear music coming from the bedroom. An assistant slowly opened the door and I entered the dark room and looked around, and in the center of the bed was a sculpture, lit from within. A giant boom box was playing Norman Greenbaum's "Spirit in the Sky."

The sculpture was a tapering silver tower made of aluminum, about three feet high, topped by a bloodred fist, the two-thumbed fist. The peyote button glowed from within with shifting colors. There was a small hole in the top of the fist where the projectile would exit. Around the base were arranged a dozen struts like the small fins on a rocket, and among these, miniature boulders.

Hunter had described a monstrous cannon, but he hadn't provided actual dimensions. It had to be of a size in keeping with his persona and his ego—huge. Johnny's cannon was 153 feet tall,

15 stories, taller even than what Hunter imagined, taller than the Statue of Liberty. It was to be built in L.A. by a prop fabrication company that could build anything you could imagine, and then shipped in pieces on flatbed trucks to Owl Farm. It would take several months to construct. It was a graceful thing, not the crude and massive pipe of Ralph's drawing, and because of that I at first had doubts, but it was truly beautiful, and it won me over.

Later in the spring I got a call from a man named Jon Equis. He was an event planner from L.A. who handled events such as the Emmy Awards and celebrity weddings. He'd been hired by Johnny to assist with the arrangements. He was coming to Denver to meet with me and see what I had in mind. He brought drawings and photos. He had gotten an aerial photo of Hunter's property at Owl Farm, with property boundaries, and had already proposed a location for the cannon and the tent. Unfortunately, it was impractical to erect the cannon on the mesa, which was an hour's hard hike up a steep roadless hillside, so we settled for the meadow that extended a good half mile behind Owl Farm. We spent a few hours talking about what the event was supposed to be, and I was insistent that it was to be a private occasion for family and close friends, and that it was a commemoration, not a party. The purpose was to honor the passing of a great man. Equis said that Johnny had told him that although he was paying for this event, it was not about him. He wanted to be informed of what was happening, but he would be in the background, and he wanted me to be happy with the result.

Over the next several months Equis and I talked frequently. What emerged was a two-part event—a private affair for friends and family that would begin as a ceremony and end as a celebration.

In the early summer the troops arrived. There was the team erecting the cannon, and there was a separate team putting together the event. Each team consisted of around eight people who flew in from L.A. and who were living in Aspen for the duration of the project. Equis rented a house a mile or so up the road from Owl Farm that became the command center. Work started early in the morning and lasted until late at night, after which there was music and drinking into the early hours. People slept on the floor or on couches. There was a cook to feed the troops. There was an art director, a logistics manager, a sound guy, a lighting person, an accountant, a few runners, a security manager, the project manager from the prop fabrication company, and several others.

In the field behind Hunter's house, there were trucks with sound equipment, lighting, a massive tent, furniture, more props brought in from L.A., carpenters, and Jon Equis in the middle of it all, keeping every detail on track.

The other team was the cannon team, assembling the massive thing, putting the final touches on the huge red fist, so large that my son and two of his friends could easily stand in the recessed area in the palm where the peyote button would be located.

In those final days, Will would get up in the morning, grab a walkie-talkie, and walk back to the building site to watch the progress. The crew would keep an eye on him, and we could always reach him on the walkie-talkie. At one point, the painter for the cannon crew painted Will's bike the same bloodred as the fist.

Throughout this entire process of planning and building, Johnny remained in the background. It was one thing for him to say this was about Hunter and not him, but to actually do it was very, very impressive, and showed me that Johnny Depp is indeed the kind of person he appears to be. He has my eternal gratitude and deep respect for all that he has done for my father. I know that he loves Hunter deeply.

On the afternoon of August 20, the day of the event, Jennifer, Will, Deb, and I walked up from the cabin toward the giant tent. The cannon was shrouded in shimmering crimson cloth, and I could hear the rhythmic pounding of the Japanese drum band playing on the small stage in front of the cannon. I knew we had succeeded in setting the right tone.

We had shuttles bring people from the parking lot at the local racetrack a few miles away. They began showing up around six p.m.

The shuttle bus drove up a newly laid gravel road from the street up to a circular drive. Guests stepped out of the bus onto a path that led to the tent. The path ran between two rows of posters with the Gonzo fist symbol facing the guests as they approached. If they looked back, they saw portraits of Hunter on the back of each poster.

Upon climbing a wide wooden staircase, they saw more framed photos of Hunter, along with portraits of some of his favorite authors, including Ernest Hemingway, Joseph Conrad, and F. Scott Fitzgerald. At the top of the stairs the guests turned right or left to walk around a wall that blocked the view of the inside of the tent. Once inside, they were in a large, dark space, with dark cloth on the walls, dark cloth covering chairs and couches, and a dark red cloth covering a circular bar in the center of the tent. The floor around the bar was painted in squares of red and blue in imitation of the floor of Hunter's kitchen. Everyone was offered a mint julep, a tribute to his Kentucky heritage, but the bar itself was closed and there were no other drinks available. By seven p.m. there were a few hundred people gathered in the tent. I took the podium and kicked off the night with a brief welcome, and then introduced a dozen or so speakers, starting with Anita, followed by Johnny Depp, Colleen Auerbach (mother of Lisl Auman), Ralph Steadman, Ed Bradley, Wayne Ewing, Jann Wenner, my wife Jennifer, Laila Nabulsi, George McGovern, George Stranahan, Tim Ferris, Bob Braudis, and Doug Brinkley. Last was a call answered by silence for Oliver Treibick. Then I spoke.

It's been six months to the day since Hunter killed himself, and I miss him like hell.

I don't know about you, but for me the grieving process has been a mysterious one, twisting and turning, arising and submerging in the most unpredictable ways. I've gotten better at just going with its flow, and it's gotten easier since then, meaning I can now feed myself and remember my phone number, which I could not do in those first several weeks. But it's not easy. And I don't think it's ever going to be easy. Tom Benton said the other day that someone asked him if this service today would give him closure, and he said "Closure! That's a Dr. Phil word. I don't want closure! I want to remember him." If anyone here is under the delusion that you will have closure at eleven p.m. tonight, I'm telling you I know it ain't so. Sorry to break the news. I'm with Tom—I don't want closure. Missing him is a way of loving him. People who have lost their parents tell me that over the years, it gets less painful, and that the sense of longing and absence is gradually balanced by fond memories and a deeper and deeper appreciation for the beloved, but no one has said that it stops hurting, or that you stop missing them. And that is as it should be.

Several people have asked me if this is what Hunter would have wanted, this cannon, this gigantic wake, these hundreds of people on his private property. First, I am finding it's dangerous and arrogant to claim to know what Hunter would have wanted, but that said, I am confident he would have been amazed and overjoyed by the monument and by the fact that not only was his request honored, but it has been honored in full measure, beyond what even he might have imagined. But, really, it doesn't matter what he would have wanted. The truth is that this night is for us, the living who miss him. It's our time to remember and share our grief, to be awestruck by the immensity of this cannon, and then to remember and share and celebrate the stories, the thousands and thousands of Hunter stories, the thousands of stories that add up to a deep love and respect for a great man and a great writer and a great friend. Not an easy man and not an easy friend, but a great one.

In the past six months, I've learned a few things. I used to think that Hunter was a cult hero, unknown to most but worshipped by a relative few. I sold him far short. Through all the letters, postcards, messages, and stories, I've begun to realize just how wide and deep his impact was on so many people. He affected far more people than we know, in far deeper ways. Hunter's writing changed people's lives, in the right ways and for the right reasons.

I've also learned just what a strong, loyal, and decent family he had here in Aspen. I can't tell you all, and you know who you are, how much your love, friendship, and support have meant to Jennifer, Will, and me. You have drawn us into your family, your tribe, and I am so deeply honored by this. Thank you. I will always carry this honor and the emblem of our tribe in my heart.

So here we go. My speaking, like this whole extravagant night, is in a way an attempt to put off acknowledging for a little longer the fact that Hunter really is gone, but gone he is, goddammit. So let's do this thing, let's shout and laugh and cry and tell stories, let's honor the great fallen warrior, the dead king, in the proper way—let us spread his ashes on Owl Farm, my father's land, the land he loved. Let us celebrate power with power. The king is dead. Long live the king.

Death and grief had been invoked, the actions of a great man related, his virtues recounted. Leaders and men of note gave tribute to him, sometimes with humor, sometimes with pathos. There was a solemn and respectful silence throughout this portion of the night.

We turned our attention to a giant projection screen and watched the end of the BBC documentary. Hunter, a youthful forty-one, described his vision of the cannon, in his trademark white L.L.Bean shorts and his bowlegged walk, pointed at the bluffs behind the house.

Then the music began; Norman Greenbaum's "Spirit in the Sky" boomed out across the meadow. The spotlights were turned on the veiled monument, and the giant crimson shroud was slowly pulled away until it was fully revealed.

It was incredible. I think everyone there was shocked at how beautiful and overwhelming it was. Some people cried, some cheered, some laughed, but mostly people responded with silent awe. The clouds hung low that night, threatening rain but never actually following through, and the spotlights cast two fist-shaped shadows on the low clouds. It was like an apparition, a Gonzo stigmata on the sky.

Ed Bastian, among other things a scholar of Tibetan Buddhism, took the small stage and read a section of Buddha's Diamond Sutra, the Prajna Paramita Sutra, in Tibetan, from a Tibetan scroll consisting of cloth strips about a foot long and a few inches wide. Ed read the ancient words with reverence. He translated what he had read into English, and it still didn't make sense to most of us, but again it didn't matter. It was his respect for the wisdom and for Hunter, by his ceremonious conduct, that inspired reverence in us, a sense that something great was transpiring, that Hunter's spirit was transforming into something timeless and grand, and we were here to witness it.

When Ed finished, the Japanese drum band resumed, six musicians standing before massive drums six feet in diameter, striking with all their might. They began slowly at first, then built gradually to a crescendo that shook our bodies and boomed into the night, bouncing off the cliffs, across the road and to the edge of the mesa a half mile away where those without invitations had gathered to watch. The drumming gradually increased in tempo and volume until it was almost unbearable, and on the final stroke, a volley of white fireworks rose in the air behind the Fist. The drummers struck again in unison, and a second curtain of light arose, this time in blue. The drummers struck a final time, and a curtain of red arose, and then a volley of shells launched from the cannon and exploded in a rapid series of white, deafening explosions. Then there was silence, and some could see a faint mist in the air, smoke and ashes, drifting down onto the ground, the tent, the crowd, and the fist, like a blessing.

After a moment of stillness, Bob Dylan's "Mr. Tambourine Man" began playing. Catharsis. People were weeping, and laughing, and cheering, they were hugging one another and whooping. They didn't know exactly what to do, but they needed to do something.

As people closest to the tent turned back, they saw that the interior had been transformed from the dark and solemn enclosure to a large, comfortable living room. The dark cloth had been removed, the circular bar had been uncovered, and low lights had been turned on, illuminating pictures and posters, along with replicas of the signs, notes, and writings that had been tacked to Hunter's kitchen walls and cupboards. There was a stuffed peacock, a wooden Morris chair, and several comfortable couches. Two refrigerators covered in black leather, in imitation of the refrigerator in Hunter's kitchen, were stocked with beer. It was an invocation of Hunter's kitchen and living room. The celebration began.

It was a memorable night even without the firing of a 153-foot cannon and the solemn speeches, the Japanese drumming, and the invocation of the Buddha's wisdom. People swamped the bar, looking for some quick relief from the intense emotions and tension of the last two hours. Lyle Lovett stepped up on the stage and sang four or five of Hunter's favorite Lovett songs, including "If I Had a Boat." When he finished, a guitarist from Dylan's band played. Throughout the night other musicians played as well, including John Oates, Jimmy Ibbotson of the Nitty Gritty Dirt Band, and David Amram. At one point Hunter's brother, Davison, climbed up on the stage with Lyle Lovett, Johnny Depp playing guitar, David Amram on flute, and the rest of the band. They did a rendition of "My Old Kentucky Home."

There was heavy drinking—as you would expect—and I heard there were other substances ingested as well. There was dancing, and flirting, and the sharing of stories from the old days.

I talked to I don't know how many people that night. I talked to old friends of Hunter's who had left Aspen twenty years ago, and the children of those friends. I talked to John Kerry, George McGovern, and Ed Bradley, and I talked to writers, bartenders, house cleaners, ranch hands, and folksingers. I thanked them all for coming, and they told me how much Hunter had meant to them. If I was lucky, they told me a story as well. I heard a number of people snuck through the tall grass from the road and managed to get into the tent.

The party went on, and on, and on. The last shuttle left around four a.m., and there were still hangers-on, mostly young people I didn't recognize. The crew started shutting down the lights around five a.m. I walked down the steps and across the dark field to the cabin feeling both exhilarated at the success of the ceremony, and sad, because now it was over, there was no other distraction that could put the grieving on hold.

Someone said the next day that the funeral was a microcosm of Hunter's life—a lot of things happened that night: there were old feuds renewed or put aside, old lovers reconnected, friendships from decades ago were renewed, there were the matching and pairing of old friends and new. It was more than a funeral for Hunter, I think. It was a toast to the good times, the wild times, not just to Hunter, but to what he represented to each person and the times that he reminded them of. Hunter was like the hub of a great wheel, connecting people who would otherwise never know each other. He was also like a magician, bringing people out of their ordinary lives into a kind of magical sphere where life was special, where you had adventures that you would remember your whole life when you finally stepped out of the magic realm back into your life. Those times would not happen again, and whether each person felt regret, relief, gratitude, melancholy, sadness, or all of them mixed together I can't say, but it was far more than a party, it was a final salute and send-off to the spirit of an era.

I thought that night that Hunter would have been proud of what we had done, and today I still believe that. He would have been proud.

ELEVEN

What Changes, What Remains the Same

Lawyers, guns, and money—Symposium—
Documentaries—The medallion

HST TIMELINE

2007   Hunter S. Thompson Symposium.
2006   *Buy the Ticket, Take the Ride* documentary released.
2008   *Gonzo: The Life and Work of Dr. Hunter S. Thompson*
          documentary released.
2011   *The Rum Diary* movie released.

I N THE NINE YEARS that have elapsed between Hunter's death and my writing these words, much has changed, and a few things have remained the same.

The first couple of years were all about Hunter. There were documentaries, interviews, lawyers, parties, books, schemes to sell this or that, phone calls from people wanting to buy Hunter's trash, weird fan art showing up in the mail, emails from strangers.

For those years I had two lives, my workaday life as an IT guy and my Hunter S. Thompson life. By the third or fourth year, though, that petered out, and life returned to something like normal.

After Hunter died, the community of which he was the hub gradually dissolved and its members moved away. George Stranahan, a steadfast Woody Creek resident for fifty years, sold his property and moved thirty miles down-valley. Ed Bastian, who had lived on the adjoining mesa, packed his bags and moved to Santa Barbara. The Craig family, the other major landowner in the valley besides Stranahan, decided to sell their property. The mad artist of Woody Creek, Michael Cleverly, was forced to move from his shack to Colorado's Western Slope. Only the die-hard residents of Lenado seem unfazed by what happened lower in the valley or the world in general. It is no longer Hunter's Woody Creek, it's an exclusive neighborhood with monstrous, multimillion-dollar houses being built where the creek used to run beneath the aspen trees and the cottonwoods. It will never become a subdivision—the minimum lot size is thirty-three acres, and besides, it's a scenic retreat for the very rich. Common suburban tract houses would not be tolerated.

Owl Farm, the land and house, are now owned by a trust administered by a large Boston law firm. I have permission to visit whenever I want and we stay in the cabin. Anita has the use of Hunter's house until she relinquishes it or dies, whichever comes first. I have not been in his house since the funeral. It was hard to accept that the land was no longer mine in the way it had been while Hunter was alive. Then I did not have to ask permission to visit. It was my home and my father's land. It is more complicated now. It is still my childhood home, but it is no longer my father's land.

Even so, it is good to be there. The meadow behind the houses is unchanged, the elk still come down to graze in the winter, the same million stars still shine hard and bright in the night sky, the peaks of the Continental Divide are still visible over the edge of the mesa opposite Owl Farm. When I walk to the top of the meadow, it is the same land, with the same scraggly juniper bushes and scrub oak on the hillside, the same red earth, the same red cliffs far behind the houses. This is still my home, it is a part of me and I am part of it. This has not changed.

I still have the medallion. To me it contains the distilled essence of my father. I will keep it always. I wear it when I want or need to invoke Hunter's spirit. If I could only choose one object of my father's to keep, it would be this.

Over the years, I've thought a lot about his suicide, why he did it, whether it was right or wrong, how I feel about it. I know he was very unhappy in his marriage, he knew he couldn't write any longer, his body was failing, he could barely walk, and he saw clearly that all these afflictions were not going to pass away, they would only get worse. I feel now, as I did then, that it was right for Hunter, and I understand why he did it. That has not changed. The way he died was consistent with how he lived—on his terms, in his time. I know he planned for Jen, Will, and me to be there with him that day, at that time. I'm grateful I was there. It would have been far worse to have gotten that phone call, to always wonder what really happened, and if I could have done anything to stop him. Because I was there I don't ask those questions.

I think about the gun he used. If that gun was offered to me, I couldn't look at it or touch it. I would bury it deep, deep in the ground someplace where it couldn't be found again or uncovered by chance, and I would forget that place, so that I could not find it again, and imagine the earth slowly eating it away, rendering it useless, dissolving it until it was only a higher concentration of iron in the red, iron-rich soil of Woody Creek. Or I would throw it into a bright forge, a giant pool of molten steel, so that it would melt and vanish, and maybe, take that image with it, that pool of blood at my father's feet, while he sat with his head slumped on his chest.

I love him and I miss him. That has not changed either. I don't think about him every day, but often. I can't say I loved him. I still love him. It would be very comforting to have a strong faith in a Christian heaven, but I do not. However, I cannot accept that he is utterly gone, no soul, nothing, only existing in people's memories. I believe, without any rational basis, that there is probably some essence out there still in some timeless, inconceivable form and that perhaps he is aware. I would like to believe that in some way he is aware of Deb, Jen, Will, and me.

I worry still whether he would approve of this or that in my life, just as I did when he was alive. Am I making the most of my life? Have I been a good steward of his legacy? It is no help to me, but he lives on as a silent judge and jury in my psyche nevertheless. His approval, even in death, is still important to me, but I know also that my approval was important to him.

I know he loves me. Over the years since his death I have not doubted that. If anything, my conviction has grown stronger. I don't have to look for the evidence, or read old letters to remind me. I just know it, I feel it. It is rooted in my being, not my head, and therefore rooted deeply and unshakably.

I am proud of him, and to be his son. That was a long time coming. When I was young, I feared and hated him. I was ashamed of him. Over many years I came to know and understand him better, to forgive him his transgressions, and then to be proud of him. I can't imagine anything could change that now.

At the end, I am left with gratitude: gratitude for the combination of luck, perseverance, blessings of the gods, the fortunate and persistent meddling of the women in our lives, the flashes of insight, willingness, and mutual need that made it possible for my father and me to heal the damage from those early years before it was too late. For this I am deeply thankful.

I am a different kind of father to my son than Hunter was to me. Jennifer, Will, and I eat dinner together every night, I go to school events, and I know the names of his friends, his teachers, how he is doing in his classes. Sometimes I lie on his bed with him at night and we talk about current events, or science, or movies. I massage his feet while the three of us watch TV. I don't go into rages; Jen and I don't scream at each other at two a.m.

I have tried to carry on what Hunter did well. I taught Will to shoot, I'm teaching him to drive. I try to let him have his own political opinions, interests, passions and desires, musical tastes and aesthetic preferences, though I may disagree with him. I want him to know that what is most important to me is that he is happy and a good man. Everything else is incidental.

I hope that I have given him reason to be proud of me as I am proud of my father. I hope that when he is thirty-five and I'm sixty-nine, we can sit together and watch *The Big Sleep* and acknowledge without speaking a mutual love and respect. I hope he knows how much I love him, the way Hunter loved me.

My son, Will, tells me he's no longer angry at Hunter for killing himself in the next room that day. He says he is mostly just sad. He misses Hunter. I miss him too. Very much. That will not change.

Honor Roll

Hunter used to include an Honor Roll in his later books. I will continue that tradition. The people on this list contributed to this book being written, whether directly in the case of my editor, Victoria Wilson, and my agent, Lynn Nesbit, whether in the form of great patience, constant support and encouragement from my family and friends, or support in the form of reading the early drafts and making recommendations. I especially want to thank Paul Scanlon for his invaluable assistance. Many others provided indirect support by playing an important supportive role in my or Hunter's life. A number of people helped keep my family and me on the rails when my father died, support for which I am forever grateful.

To all of you, thank you, from the bottom of my heart, for helping to make this book possible.

Jennifer Winkel Thompson
Will Thompson
Deb Fuller
Lynn Nesbit
Victoria Wilson

Jann Wenner
Paul Scanlon
Tom Gilboy
Johnny Depp
Christi Dembrowski

Norm Todd
John Equis
Joel Mandel
Hal Haddon
Doug Brinkley
Loren Jenkins
Kevin Breslin
Ed Bastian
Tim Ferris
Ralph and Anna Steadman
Richard Brennan
Sandra Wright (previously
    Thompson)
Hal Wakefield
Jimmy Buffett
Jane Buffett
Tom Corcoran
Tom Benton
Betty Benton
Brian and Michelle Benton
Marci Benton
Doris Kearns and Dick Goodwin
Oliver Treibick
Laila Nabulsi
Bob and Gabby Rafelson
Brad Laboe
Carol and Palmer Hood
George and Patty Stranahan
Cliff Little
Rhett Harper
Ann Dowell
Nicole Fulcher
Virginia Thompson
Davison and Adelaide Thompson
Robin, Adelaide Hunter, and
    Susannah Thompson
Patrick Krause
Chrissy Sawtelle
John, Kristi, Jack, and Will
    Doherty
Andrea Winkel Haines
Paul Haines

Ella and Will Haines
Carrie Watson and Phil
    Fontana
Ellis and Madelyn Fontana
Pamela Reich
Jack Thibeau
Gene McGarr
Debra Wilde
Marla Bonds
Shannon Jones
Lyle Lovett
Julie Conklin
Bob Braudis
Joey DiSalvo
Jeff Armstrong
Ed Bradley
Patricia Blanchet
Dana Krafchik
Tami Hogan
Alisa Winkel
Pete Laborde
Tory Read
David Grinspoon
David Monsma
Walter Isaacson
Alex Gibney
Trish, Steve, and Hayden Setlik
The Tiberi family
Dede Brinkman
Todd Divel
Eddie Mize
Bill Murray
Don Stober
Gerry and Chris Goldstein
Dan Dibble
Michael Cleverly
Cass Cleverly
John Zajicek
Jeff Kass
Marea Evans
Nicole Lefavour
Stevens Brosnihan

A NOTE ON THE TYPE

*This book was set in Adobe Garamond. Designed for the Adobe
Corporation by Robert Slimbach, the fonts are based on types first cut by
Claude Garamond (ca. 1480–1561). Garamond was a pupil of Geoffroy
Tory and is believed to have followed the Venetian models, although
he introduced a number of important differences, and it is to him that
we owe the letter we now know as "old style." He gave to his letters a
certain elegance and feeling of movement that won their creator an
immediate reputation and the patronage of Francis I of France.*

COMPOSED BY *North Market Street Graphics, Lancaster, Pennsylvania*

PRINTED AND BOUND BY *Berryville Graphics, Berryville, Virginia*

DESIGNED BY *Iris Weinstein*